Jürgen Grothe (Hrsg.)

The End of the War
and a New Beginning
in Berlin

Kriegsende und Neubeginn in Berlin

Jaron Verlag

Foto S. 1: Kurz nach Ende des Kriegs (Juli 1945) – Flüchtlinge aus dem Osten campieren vor dem Brandenburger Tor
Foto S. 72: Neubeginn (um 1955) – Als die Zeit des »Wirtschaftswunders« begann, ließ es sich im »Ballhaus Resi« an der Hasenheide gut flirten

Originalausgabe
1. Auflage 2007

Übersetzung: Miriamne Fields, Berlin
Fotos: Landesarchiv Berlin
Umschlaggestaltung: Atelier Kattner, Berlin, unter Verwendung eines Fotos des Landesarchivs Berlin (Gelände des ehemaligen Fremdenverkehrshauses an der Potsdamer Straße, 1949)
Satz: Jaron Verlag GmbH, Berlin
Lithographie: LVD GmbH, Berlin
Druck und Bindung: Westermann Druck Zwickau

ISBN 978-3-89773-558-3

Ende und Anfang

Berlin liegt im Dunkel der Nacht. Kein Lichtstrahl fällt aus den Fenstern der Häuser auf die Straßen. Verdunkelung ist angeordnet. Nicht der kleinste Lichtschein soll den Bombern zeigen, wo die Straßen und Plätze liegen, die Häuser stehen. Der Krieg der Bomben ist auf die Stadt zurückgefallen, von der er ausgegangen war.
Sirenen heulen, Menschen hasten mit wenigen Habseligkeiten aus ihren Wohnungen in die Luftschutzkeller oder Bunker. Die Wohnungstüren müssen geöffnet bleiben. Der Luftschutzwart achtet darauf, dass die Vorschriften eingehalten werden und alle Bewohner ihre Wohnungen verlassen haben. Scheinwerfer suchen den Himmel ab, das Motorengebrumm der Bomber ist zu hören, nähert sich, dem Pfeifen der fallenden Bomben und Luftminen folgen der Einschlag und die Explosion, selbst Häuser, die nicht getroffen werden, wackeln in sich. Die Menschen sitzen mit ernsten Mienen auf Stühlen und Bänken. Angst zeichnet ihre Gesichter. Bei jedem Fliegeralarm stellt sich die gleiche Frage: Trifft es diesmal uns?
Im Januar und März 1943 beginnen die Briten mit groß angelegten Flächen-

The End and the Beginning

Berlin lies in the darkness of the night. No light seeps through the windows of the buildings onto the street. The blacking out order has been issued. Not even the smallest ray of light should allow the bombs to recognize where streets and plazas are located or where buildings stand. The war of bombs now fall back on the city that began it.
Sirens cry and the people scurry from their apartments into the air-raid shelters and bunkers, carrying with them a few personal possessions. The doors of the apartments must be left open. The air-raid warden pays attention to whether the regulations are followed properly and makes sure that all the residents have left their apartments. Spotlights search the sky. You can hear the hum of the bombers as they come closer. The whistle of the bombs and aerial mines is followed by the moment of impact and then the explosion. Even the buildings that aren't directly hit shake and rattle. The people sit on chairs and benches with grave expressions on their faces. They repeatedly ask themselves the same question during every air-raid warning. Will we be hit this time?

1940: In einem Luftschutzkeller lächelt man für den Fotografen. So eng wie in diesem Keller in der Prager Straße 29 in Wilmersdorf war es in den meisten Schutzeinrichtungen.

1940: Smiles for the photographer in an air-raid bunker. Most of the air-raid facilities were crowded like this one at Prager Strasse 29 in Wilmersdorf.

1943: Luftschutztrupp in Berlin-Mitte beim Löschen nach einem Bombenangriff der Briten. So sah es in vielen Straßen nach der Entwarnung aus.

1943: Air-raid protection troops in Berlin-Mitte extinguish a fire after a bombing. This is how many streets looked after the all-clear signal was sounded.

6.10.1944: Der brennende Turm der Nikolaikirche nach einem Luftangriff. Derartige Fotos aufzunehmen war streng verboten. Der Fotograf Karl Schultz war auf das Dach eines Hauses in der Breite Straße gestiegen.

6.10.1944: The burning tower of the Nikolai Church after an air raid. The photographer Karl Schultz took this illegal photograph from the roof of a building on Breite Strasse.

bombardements auf die Innenstadt. Kaum sind die Straßen von den Trümmern geräumt, kommt der nächste Bombenteppich, und die Aufräumungsarbeiten fangen von vorn an. Im März 1944 beginnen dann die Amerikaner mit ihren Tagesangriffen. Der schwerste erfolgt am 3.Februar 1945, kurz nach 11 Uhr: Die U.S. Air Force schickt 937 viermotorige Flying Fortresses (»Fliegende Festungen«) nach Berlin, begleitet von 600 Jagdflugzeugen. In etwa 50 Minuten werden 2000 Tonnen Spreng- und 250 Tonnen Phosphor-Brandbomben abgeworfen. Ziel ist die Zerstörung der Berliner Innenstadt.
Die erste Bombenwelle richtet sich gegen die Umgebung des Askanischen und des Potsdamer Platzes, die zweite gegen das Zeitungs- und das Regierungsviertel. Zerstört werden der Anhalter und der Potsdamer Bahnhof, Teile der Wilhelmstraße, das Schloss, der Dom, das Opernhaus Unter den Linden und die Altstadt um die Nikolaikirche, aus den Türmen der Kirchen am Gen-

In January and March of 1943 the British begin with widespread carpet bombing of the city center. As soon as the streets have been cleared of rubble, the next carpet bombing occurs and the clearing up begins all over again. In March 1944, the Americans begin with their daytime attacks. The worst one occurs on February 3, 1945, shortly after 11 a.m.: The U.S. Air Force sends 937 four-motor Flying Fortresses to Berlin, accompanied by 600 pursuit planes. Within about fifty minutes 2000 tons of explosive and 250 tons of fire bombs are dropped. The goal is to destroy the Berlin city center.
The first set of bombs is aimed at the neighborhoods around the Askanische Platz and Potsdamer Platz; the second one targets the newspaper and government quarters. The Anhalter and Potsdamer stations are destroyed along with parts of Wilhelmstrasse, the palace, the cathedral, the opera house on Unter den Linden and the old city around the Nikolai Church. Flames blaze

darmenmarkt lodern die Flammen. Nach diesen Bombenabwürfen ist die Berliner Innenstadt ein Inferno aus Flammen und Trümmern. Der Himmel ist verdunkelt von den Rauchschwaden. Ruß und ein feiner Regen aus Asche fällt auf die Straßen, Häuser und Ruinen. Überall ist das Schreien der Verwundeten oder Verschütteten zu hören. Nach dem Abzug der Rauchschwaden bietet sich dem Betrachter ein makabres Bild: Anstelle der Regierungsbauten und Bankpaläste sowie der mondänen Geschäfte ragen bizarre Ruinen in den Himmel.

Nach dem 421. Luftalarm stellen die Briten und Amerikaner am 21. April 1945 die Bombardements auf Berlin ein. Die Lufthoheit geht in die Verantwortung der sowjetischen Jagdflieger über, die die Bodenoffensive der Roten Armee unterstützen.

Am selben Tag erreichen die sowjetischen Armeen den Verteidigungsgürtel Berlins. Die Stadt ist am Tag zuvor in den Belagerungszustand versetzt worden. Schwache Truppenteile, Volkssturm und Hitlerjugend, darunter Vierzehnjährige, stellen sich der Übermacht der sowjetischen Verbände entgegen. Kämpfe entwickeln sich in der Linie Pankow, Lichtenberg, Niederschönhausen und Frohnau. Am 23.4. erobern sowjetische Truppen Köpenick, Frohnau und Teile des Bezirks Pankow. Am 26.4. ist Berlin von sowjetischen Truppen der 1. Bjelorussischen Front unter Marschall Shukow und der 1. Ukrainischen Front unter Marschall Konjew eingeschlossen. Aber die Stadt wird nicht übergeben: Hitler hofft auf die 12. Armee unter General Wenck, der von der Elbe bis nach Ferch vorstieß, dort aber im sowjetischen Feuer steckenblieb. Am 27.4. besetzen die sowjetischen Truppen Spandau, und im Süden dringen sie in die Bezirke Schöneberg und Kreuzberg ein. Von Norden her besetzen sie Charlottenburg, und über das Tempelhofer Feld erreichen sie den inneren Verteidigungsring der Stadt. Am Halleschen Tor und am Alexanderplatz beginnt der Endkampf um die Innenstadt Berlins. Nach der Besetzung weiterer Stadtteile wird am 28.4. Generaloberst Nikolaij E. Bersarin zum ersten Stadtkommandanten von Berlin ernannt. Die Rote Armee erobert Kreuzberg, Wilmersdorf und endgültig Spandau.

Am 30.4.1945 nimmt sich Adolf Hitler, der sich „Führer“ nannte und Gehorsam bis zum Letzten verlangte, im Bunker der Reichskanzlei das Leben. Nicht weit

April 1945: Die sowjetischen Panzerspitzen haben in Weißensee Berlin erreicht. Joseph Goebbels erlässt am 23.4.1945 den Befehl: »Berlin wird bis zum Letzten verteidigt …«

April 1945: The first Soviet tanks reach Berlin in Weissensee. On 23.4.1945 Joseph Goebbels issues the order for "Berlin to be defended to the end..."

April 1945: Schwere sowjetische Granatwerfer an der »Hauptkampflinie« in der Schöneberger Hauptstraße. Im Hintergrund sind die Häuser Hauptstraße 19 und 20 zu sehen.

April 1945: Heavy Soviet artillery on the "main battle line" at Haupt strasse in Schöneberg. The buildings at Hauptstrasse 19 and 20 are visi ble in the background.

6.5.1945: Der Befehlshaber des Verteidigungsbereiches Berlin, General Weidling, verlässt den Bunker der Reichkanzlei. Laut sowjetischer Propaganda war es die Gefangennahme Weidlings am 2. Mai.

6.5.1945: General Weidling, commander of the Berlin defense area, lea ves the bunker of the Reich Chancellery. According to Soviet propa ganda, it was the day of his arrest on May 2.

from the churches on Gendarmenmarkt. After these bombings the Berlin city center is an inferno of flames and rubble. The sky is darkened by the drifting smoke. Soot and ashes rain down lightly on the streets, buildings and ruins. Screams are heard from everywhere: people are injured or buried beneath the rubble. As the smoke fades, the survivors see a macabre picture: Instead of government buildings, bank palaces and fancy shops, a bizarre landscape of ruins stretch up into the sky.

The British and Americans end their bombardment of Berlin after the 421st air-raid alarm on April 21, 1945. The Soviet pursuit planes take charge of the skies and assist the Red Army ground offensive.

On the same day the Soviet army reaches the defense belt of Berlin. The city was placed under siege the day before. Weak German troop formations, Volkssturm units of old men, and the Hitler Youth – among them 14-year-old boys – face the far-superior Soviet troops. Fighting takes place on the Pankow, Lichtenberg, Niederschönhausen and Frohnau battle lines. On April 23, the Soviet troops conquer Köpenick, Frohnau und parts of the Pankow district. On April 26, Berlin is encircled by Soviet troops of the 1st Belorussian front commanded by Marshal Zhukov and the 1st Ukrainian front under Marshal Konev. But the city is not surrendered. Hitler still hopes for the 12th army under General Wenck, which is advancing from the Elbe to Ferch, but was caught in Soviet fire. On April 27, the Soviet troops occupy Spandau and break into the Schöneberg and Kreuzberg districts in the south. From the north they occupy Charlottenburg and reach the inner defense ring of the city from across the Tempelhofer Field. The final battles for the city center begin at Hallesche Tor and Alexanderplatz. On April 28, after the Soviets have occupied other sections of the city, Senior General Nikolai E. Bersarin is appointed City Commander of Berlin. The Red Army conquers Kreuzberg, Wilmersdorf and finally Spandau.

On April 30, 1945, Adolf Hitler, who called himself the "Führer" and demanded total obedience up to the very end, commits suicide in the bunker of the Reich Chancellery. On the very same day, not far from there, the Red Army hoists the red flag onto the roof of the Reichstag building as a symbol of their victory.

entfernt, auf dem Dach des Reichstagsgebäudes, hissen am selben Tag Soldaten der Roten Armee die Rote Fahne als Zeichen des Sieges.
Im Haus Schulenburgring 2 in Tempelhof unterzeichnet am 2.5. der deutsche Stadtkommandant von Berlin, Generalleutnant Helmuth Weidling, den ihm vom sowjetischen Generaloberst Tschuikow vorgelegten Kapitulationsbefehl für die Berliner Garnison. In den Morgenstunden des gleichen Tages hatte ein SS-Kommando noch den S-Bahntunnel unter dem Landwehrkanal gesprengt; unzählige verwundete Soldaten und Zivilisten ertranken. Am 4.5. meldet das Oberkommando der deutschen Wehrmacht das Ende des Kampfes um Berlin.
Nach dem Ende der Kriegshandlungen und dem Erscheinen der ersten Zeitungen wird vielen Berlinern erst das erschreckende Ausmaß des Krieges bewusst. In der »Täglichen Rundschau«, seit dem 15.5. von der Roten Armee herausgegeben, wird erstmals ausführlich über die Konzentrationslager berichtet.
Im Gebäude der ehemaligen Pionierschule in Karlshorst unterzeichnen am 8.5. im Namen des Oberkommandos der Wehrmacht Generalfeldmarschall Keitel, Generaladmiral von Friedeburg und Generaloberst Stumpff in Anwesenheit des Marschalls der Sowjetunion Shukow, des britischen Luftmarschalls Tedder, des Befehlshabers der strategischen Luftstreitkräfte der Vereinigten Staaten, General Spaatz, sowie des Oberbefehlshabers der französischen Armee Lattre de Tassigny die Urkunde über die bedingungslose Kapitulation der deutschen Wehrmacht.

Berlin, diese einst vor Leben sprühende Stadt, war schwer angeschlagen. Sie glich einem riesigen Trümmerhaufen. Die sinnlosen Endkämpfe in den Straßen mit ihrem Artilleriebeschuss hatte das Vernichtungswerk der Bomben vollendet. In der Stadt waren 27 679 Gebäude total zerstört, 20 127 schwer beschädigt, 22 848 galten als reparierbar, 171 965 waren leicht beschädigt.
In die Trauer über das Verlorene mischte sich der Trotz. Anstatt lange zu jammern, packte man an. Die fast vergessenen Trümmerfrauen waren es, die das neue Berlin entstehen ließen. Sie waren es, die die Straßen ohne technische Hilfsmittel vom Schutt der Ruinen befreiten und die noch brauchbaren Ziegelsteine zur Verwendung an Neubauten putzten.
Doch es kam nicht zu der gewünschten ruhigen politischen Entwicklung in Europa. Dem Zweiten Weltkrieg folgte der »Kalte Krieg« zweier verfeindeter Weltanschauungen. Und ins Zentrum dieses Spannungsfelds rückte schon bald Berlin.
Die Stadt war in vier Sektoren aufgeteilt worden. Zum Sowjetischen Sektor gehörten die Bezirke Mitte, Prenzlauer Berg, Friedrichshain, Treptow, Köpenick, Lichtenberg, Weißensee und Pankow, zum Amerikanischen Sektor Kreuzberg, Zehlendorf, Schöneberg und Steglitz, zum Britischen Tiergarten,

Juli 1945: Sowjetische Soldatinnen demonstrieren an der Ecke Unter den Linden / Wilhelmstraße die Präsenz der Besatzungsmacht – und regeln den nicht vorhandenen Verkehr.

July 1945: Female Soviet soldiers draw attention to the presence of the occupying powers on the corner of Unter den Linden / Wilhelmstrasse – by directing non-existent traffic.

In the building at Schulenburgring 2 in Tempelhof, Lieutenant General Helmuth Weidling, the German City Commander of Berlin, signs the capitulation for the Berlin garrison that is presented to him by the Soviet Major General Chuikov on May 2. In the early morning hours of the same day an SS commando blows up an urban railway tunnel under the Landwehr Canal; countless wounded soldiers and civilians drown. On April 4, the high command of the German Army announces the end of the battle for Berlin.
Many Berliners do not realize the horrendous magnitude of the war until after the fighting has ceased and the first newspapers are printed. The first detailed reports on the concentration camps appear in the "Täglichen Rundschau" newspaper, published by the Red Army as of May 15.
On May 8, in the former pioneer school in Karlshorst, General Field Marshal Keitel, Grand Admiral von Friedeburg and Colonel General Stumpff sign the document stating the unconditional surrender of the German army on behalf of the high command of the German army and in the presence of Soviet Marshal Zhukov, British Air Marshal Tedder, United States Strategic Air Force Commander General Spaatz, and Commander of the French Army Lattre de Tassigny.

Berlin, once a city bubbling over with life, was badly beaten. After the war it resembled a huge heap of rubble. The artillery fire of the senseless final battles fought on the streets of Berlin finished off the mass destruction that was caused by the bombs. A total of 27,679 buildings were completely destroyed, 20,127 were heavily damaged, 22,848 were considered reparable and 171,965 were only slightly damaged.
The sadness over all that was lost was mixed with feelings of defiance. Instead of whining, Berliners got to work. The women who cleared the rubble, nearly forgotten today, made a new Berlin possible. They were the ones who removed the debris of ruins from the streets without the help of any technical machinery. They were the ones who cleaned off the bricks so that they could be used again for new buildings.
But the hope that a peaceful political climate would settle in Europe was dashed. World War II was followed by the Cold War fought by two hostile world ideologies. And Berlin soon emerged at the center of the conflict.
The city was divided into four sectors. The districts of Mitte, Prenzlauer Berg, Friedrichshain, Treptow, Köpenick, Lichtenberg, Weißensee and Pankow belonged to the Soviet sector. The American sector included the districts of Kreuzberg, Zehlendorf, Schöneberg and Steglitz. The British controlled the Tiergarten, Charlottenburg, Spandau and Wilmersdorf districts. The British handed over the districts of Wedding and Reinickendorf to the French.
1948 was a year of crisis. On March 3 the Soviets walked out of the Allied Control Council and on July 1 they left the Allied commander headquarters. On June 24, 1948, the Soviet military administration responded to the cur-

Charlottenburg, Spandau, Wilmersdorf, die Bezirke Wedding und Reinickendorf hatten die Briten den Franzosen übergeben.
Es kam das Krisenjahr 1948. Am 20.3. verließen die Sowjets den Alliierten Kontrollrat, am 1.7. die Alliierte Kommandantur. Auf die Währungsreform, die Berlin in Ost- und Westmark-Bezirke teilte, antwortete die sowjetische Militärverwaltung am 24.6.1948 mit der Sperrung sämtlicher Zufahrtswege nach West-Berlin. Während der Blockade, die bis zum 12.5.1949 dauerte, wurde West-Berlin durch die westlichen Alliierten über die Luftbrücke mit lebenswichtigen Gütern versorgt. Am 7.10.1949 erklärte die SED den Sowjetischen Sektor Berlins zur Hauptstadt der Deutschen Demokratischen Republik. Fast ein Jahr später trat für West-Berlin eine neue Verfassung in Kraft, die besagte, dass Berlin gleichzeitig Stadt und Land ist; eine Eingliederung in die Bundesrepublik verhinderte der Viermächtestatus. Den Höhepunkt der Spaltung markiert der Bau der Sperrmauer am 13.8.1961: Der erste Arbeiter- und Bauernstaat auf deutschem Boden sperrte seine Bewohner ein, trennte Familien voneinander.
Das politische Leben begann bereits am 13.5.1945 mit der Einsetzung von Dr. Arthur Werner zum Oberbürgermeister von Groß-Berlin durch den sowjetischen Stadtkommandanten Generaloberst Bersarin, am 19.5. folgte die Einführung der Mitglieder des Magistrats im sog. Neuen Stadthaus in der Parochialstraße. Am 10.6.1945 wurde durch Befehl Nr. 2 des Obersten Chefs der Sowjetischen Militäradministration die Gründung und Tätigkeit demokratischer Parteien und Organisationen erlaubt. Einen Tag später nahm die KPD ihre Tätigkeit auf, bald folgten SPD, CDU und LDP. Die Zwangsvereinigung der beiden Arbeiterparteien scheiterte in Berlin am Widerstand der SPD-Mitglieder. Der Zusammenschluss beider Parteien im Ostteil der Stadt konnte jedoch nicht verhindert werden. Am 14.4.1946 kam es zur Gründung der Sozialistischen Einheitspartei Deutschlands, kurz SED.
Wie vereinbart rückten am 4.7.1945 die amerikanischen, britischen und französischen Besatzungstruppen in die ihnen zugewiesenen Bezirke ein.
Am 15.5. erschien mit der »Täglichen Rundschau« die erste deutschsprachige Tageszeitung, herausgegeben von der sowjetischen Armee, ebenso wie die »Berliner Zeitung«, die am 21.5. erstmals herauskam. »Der Tagesspiegel« folgte am 27.9. Bereits ab 4.5. war der Berliner Rundfunk wieder zu hören. Am 4.9.1946 nahm der »Rundfunk im Amerikanischen Sektor«, kurz RIAS, seine Sendungen auf. Auch Konzerte und Theateraufführungen wurden ab Mai 1945 wieder veranstaltet. Erste Kunstausstellungen fanden im Juni in der Aula der Handelsschule in der Halleschen Straße und durch die »Kammer der Kunstschaffenden beim Magistrat« – mit Werken von Carl Hofer, Max Beckmann, Erst Ludwig Kirchner, Max Pechstein, Max Kaus, Richard Scheibe und anderen – statt. Durch die stark zerstören Anlagen des Zoologischen Gartens konnte der Besucher wieder seit dem 1. Juli wandeln, und in Karlshorst fand am gleichen Tag das erste Trabrennen statt. Am 14.5. fuhren die ersten U-Bahn-Züge auf den Strecken Hermannplatz—Bergstraße und Schönleinstraße—Boddinstraße.
Ein riesiges Problem, das über Jahre nicht gelöst werden konnte, stellte der Schulunterricht dar. Es herrschte Hunger, es fehlte Kleidung, es fehlte Brennmaterial. Im November 1945 begann im Kampf gegen die Unterernährung der Kinder die Ausgabe der Schulspeise. Die Schulgebäude waren zerstört, be-

rency reform, which established two different forms of money in the east and west districts, by blocking all access routes to West Berlin. During the blockade, which lasted until May 12, 1949, the Western Allies delivered all necessary goods to West Berlin through an airlift. On October 7, 1949, the SED, the Socialist Unity Party which ruled in the eastern part of Berlin, declared the Soviet sectors of Berlin to be the capital of the German Democratic Republic. Almost a year later a new constitution came into effect in West Berlin that established Berlin as both a city and a state. The four-power-status prevented it from being integrated into the Federal Republic.
The construction of the Berlin Wall on August 13, 1961 marked the culmination of the city's division: The first "State of the Workers and Farmers" (the SED term for East Germany) to exist on German territory confined its own population and divided families.
Political life re-established itself by May 13, 1945 when Dr. Arthur Werner was appointed mayor of Greater Berlin by the Soviet City Commander, Senior General Bersarin. On May 19, members of the Berlin municipal authority convened in the Neue Stadthaus on Parochialstrasse. On June 10, 1945, senior head of the Soviet military administration issued order no. 2, which allowed for the establishment and activity of democratic political parties and organizations. One day later the KPD (German Communist Party) became active, the SPD (German Socialist Party), CDU (Christian Democratic Union) and LPD (Liberal Democratic Party) followed soon after. In the west of Berlin, the forced unification of the two workers' parties failed due to resistance from SPD members. But in the eastern part of the city this union could not be prevented. On April 14, 1946 the Socialist Unity Party, abbreviated SED, was established.
As agreed, the American, British and French occupying troops moved into their designated sectors on July 7, 1945.
The first German newspaper, the "Täglichen Rundschau", appeared on May 15. It was published by the Soviet army as was the "Berliner Zeitung", which appeared for the first time on May 21. "Der Tagesspiegel" followed on September 27. By May 4, Berlin radio was on the air again. On September 4, 1946, »Radio in the American Sector,« RIAS for short, began its broadcasting. Concerts and theater performances took place in May 1945. The first art exhibitions took place in June in the auditorium of the trade school on Hallesche Strasse, organized by the "Municipal Authority's Chamber of Creators of Art." It presented works by Carl Hofer, Max Beckmann, Ernst Ludwig Kirchner, Max Pechstein, Max Kaus, Richard Scheibe and many others. By July 1, visitors could stroll through the badly damaged grounds of the Zoological Gardens, and on the same day the first trotting races took place in Karlhorst. On May 14, the first subway trains were running between Hermannplatz and Bergstrasse and between Schönleinstrasse and Boddinstrasse.
Schooling in Berlin posed a major problem that wasn't solved for many years. People were hungry, lacked suitable clothing and fuel for heat. In November 1945 schools began serving meals to schoolchildren to prevent their undernourishment. The school buildings were either destroyed, damaged or ravaged. Of the 608 school buildings that existed in 1938, only 292 could be used temporarily. The teaching staff posed an additional problem. The educational ideas of the older teachers, trained under National Socialism, were now obso-

schädigt oder verwüstet. Von den 608 Schulgebäuden, die es im Jahr 1938 gab, konnten nur noch 292 behelfsmäßig genutzt werden. Ein besonderes Problem waren die Lehrkräfte. Das nationalsozialistische Erziehungsgut der alten Lehrer war obsolet. 55 Prozent aller Lehrer waren Schulhelfer, Hilfslehrer oder »Neulehrer«, wie die im Anschluss an das Kriegsabitur in Kurzlehrgängen ausgebildeten Pädagogen genannt wurden. Noch ohne jegliche Berufserfahrung, sollten sie den Schülerinnen und Schülern die neuen Ideen der Demokratie vermitteln. 1947 fehlten immer noch 6310 Klassenzimmer. So fand der Unterricht teilweise in drei Schichten statt. In den Eiswintern 1945/46 und 1946/47, als die Temperaturen teilweise unter minus 30 Grad lagen, mussten die Schüler Brennmaterial für provisorische Öfen mitbringen. 1948 wurde die erste neue Schule errichtet: in der Singerstraße 8a im Bezirk Mitte. Der erste Schulneubau im Westteil der Stadt erfolgte 1949 an der Waldschulallee 83 in Charlottenburg.

Mit der Wirtschaft war es schlecht bestellt. Die Demontage vor allem West-Berliner Wirtschafts- und Industriebetriebe wie Osram, Siemens, Borsig und der AEG durch die sowjetische Armee erreichte ihren Höhepunkt kurz vor dem Einmarsch der Truppen der drei Westalliierten. In West-Berlin wurden 85 Prozent der Industrieanlagen demontiert, im Sowjetischen Sektor 33 Prozent. Für den Wiederaufbau des Wohnraumes oder gar Neubauten fehlten wesentliche Voraussetzungen: Geld und Baumaterial. Für den Westteil der Stadt kam noch die isolierte Lage hinzu. In der Frankfurter Allee im Bezirk Friedrichshain, der Straße, die während des Zweiten Weltkrieges fast völlig zerstört worden war, wurde im Februar 1946 mit dem ersten Bauabschnitt zur Errichtung von 1200 Wohnungen begonnen.

Der eigentliche Wiederaufbau begann dort allerdings erst 1949. Am 21.12. erhielt die gesamte Straße den Namen Stalinallee. Die sich beiderseits der auf 90 Meter verbreiterten Straße erstreckenden Wohnblöcke wurden von unterschiedlichen Architekten mit ihren Kollektiven in traditioneller Bauweise errichtet. Die erste sozialistische Straße in Deutschland wurde eine Prachtstraße im Architekturstil der Stalin-Ära.

Im Kontrast zur Stalinallee standen die Neubauten im Hansaviertel, die den städtebaulichen und architektonischen Neubeginn im Westen der Stadt markierten. Sie sind ein Beispiel für die internationale Moderne. Mit seiner aufgelockerten Bauweise demonstrierte das Hansaviertel die Abkehr von der Mietkaserne der Kaiserzeit, aber auch der Monumentalarchitektur der 1930er Jahre und eben auch der Bebauung der Stalinallee.

An den Neubauten innerhalb der Internationalen Bauausstellung 1957, kurz »Interbau«, beteiligten sich zahlreiche namhafte Architekten aus der ganzen Welt. Die offene, von Grünanlagen umgebene Bebauung galt als Symbol für die freiheitliche, demokratische, westliche Gesellschaft.

Berlin 1945 bis Mitte der 50er Jahre: Das war Zerstörung und Leid, aber auch tatkräftiger Neuanfang. Die Fotos sind unbestechliche Zeitzeugnisse. Sie begleiten die Geschichte einer Stadt, die Besonderes zu erleiden hatte und Besonderes leistete. So sind sie eine Botschaft gegen das Vergessen.

lete. Fifty-five percent of all teachers were school assistants, assistant teachers or "new teachers," which was the term used for educators who were in possession of a secondary school "war diploma," and had received brief pedagogical training. Despite their total lack of work experience, they were expected to convey to schoolchildren the new ideas of democracy. In 1947, 6310 classrooms were still needed. Sometimes it was necessary to conduct class in three separate shifts. In the icy winter of 1945/46 and 1946/47, with temperatures sometimes going as low as 30 degrees below zero Celsius, students had to bring their own fuel to heat the provisional ovens. In 1948 the first new school was built at Singerstrasse 8a in the Mitte district. The first new school in the western part of the city was built in 1949 at Waldschulallee 83 in Charlottenburg.

The economic situation was also difficult. The Soviet army had dismantled factory equipment in most of West Berlin's economic and industrial facilities such as Osram, Siemens, Borsig and the AEG. This dismantling reached its highpoint just shortly before the three Western Allied troops marched into Berlin. In West Berlin, 85% of the industrial equipment was stripped down in comparison to 33% in the Soviet sectors.

Money and building materials, the two basic prerequisites for reconstructing residential buildings or erecting new ones, were totally lacking. The western part of the city had the added difficulty of being physically isolated from West Germany. In the East in the Friedrichshain district, the first phase of construction for 1200 new buildings began in February 1946 on Frankfurter Allee, a street that was almost completely destroyed during World War II.

But the real reconstruction did not begin until 1949. On December 21 the entire street was given the name Stalinallee. It was widened to ninety meters and residential blocks were erected in the traditional building style on both sides by different architects and their collectives. The first "socialist street in Germany" became a boulevard in the architectural style of the Stalin era.

New buildings were also erected in the Hansa Quarter, marking a new beginning of urban planning and architectural designs in the western part of the city. Providing a strong contrast to the Stalinallee, they are an example of international modernity. With its unregimented building style, the Hansa Quarter demonstrated a departure from the tenement buildings of Imperial Germany, from the monumental architecture of the 1930s and from the buildings on Stalinallee.

Many famous architects from all over the world participated in creating new buildings for the International Building Exhibition of 1957, called "Interbau" for short. The open developments, enclosed by green areas, were a symbol of free, democratic, western society.

Berlin from 1945 to the mid-1950s: These were years of destruction and anguish, but also of an energetic new beginning. These photographs provide unerring proof of this. They accompany the history of a city that endured, but also accomplished so much. And thus they are also a memory against forgetting.

1945

Relikte des untergegangenen Regimes: Flugzeuge der deutschen Luftwaffe, die von den amerikanischen Truppen 1945 auf dem Zentralflughafen Tempelhof vorgefunden wurden. Die ausgedehnten Flughafengebäude, ab 1934 nach Plänen von Ernst Sagebiel erbaut, hatten während des Krieges erhebliche Schäden erlitten. Am 2.7.1945 übernahmen die amerikanischen Behörden die in ihrem Sektor liegende Anlage. Am 20.5.1946 wurde der militärische, am 9.7.1951 der zivile Flugverkehr wiederaufgenommen.

Relicts of the collapsed regime: Airplanes of the German air force that were discovered by American troops at the Tempelhof central airport in 1945. The expansive airport buildings, built in 1934 from plans designed by Ernst Sagebiel, suffered major damage during the war. On July 7, 1945 the American authorities took over the facilities that were located in their sector. The Tempelhof Central airport was re-opened to military air travel on May 20, 1946. Civilian air travel recommenced on July 9, 1951.

▷ Am Wilhelmplatz, der 1936 zum Aufmarschplatz umgestaltet worden war, lag die nationalsozialistische Zentrale der Macht. Hier ließ sich der »Führer« feiern. Das Foto zeigt die Ecke Wilhelmstraße/Vossstraße mit Palais Borsig und, rechts daneben, Reichskanzlei. 1935 ließ Adolf Hitler für seine Selbstinszenierungen durch Albert Speer den Balkon anbauen. – Dieses Plakat mit einem Ausspruch Hitlers, nach Kriegsende 1945 an der Ruine des Hauses Reinickendorfer Str. 4 aufgehängt, macht den Wahnsinn der NS-Politik sinnfällig.

▷ *The National Socialist power headquarters at Wilhelmplatz, which was converted into marching grounds in 1936. This is where the Führer was celebrated. The photo shows the corner of Wilhelmstrasse/Vossstrasse with the Borsig Palace and the Reich Chancellery to the right. Adolf Hitler had Albert Speer add a balcony in 1935 to aid his public image – This poster with a Hitler quote ("Give me ten years and you won't recognize Germany"), which hung on the ruins of a building, illustrates the madness of the Nazi policies.*

Juni 1946

1945

1945

Notfriedhöfe waren nach dem Ende der Kampfhandlungen vielerorts in Berlin anzutreffen. Ob auf den Höfen der Wohnhäuser oder an den Ufern der Havel – überall standen Kreuze zur Erinnerung an meist unbekannte Tote. Noch 1945 erfolgten die Umbettungen auf städtische Friedhöfe. Das Foto zeigt einen Notfriedhof am Nollendorfplatz, dem Mittelpunkt des »Berliner Westens«. Der Hochbahnhof Nollendorfplatz mit seiner wie eine Kaiserkrone aussehenden Kuppel und einem Brunnen war zur Ruine geworden, der Bahnsteig lag auf der Straße.

Many make-shift cemeteries could be found in Berlin after the fighting had ceased. Crosses in memory of the dead (mostly unidentified) were everywhere – in residential courtyards and on the banks of the Havel River. In 1945 the corpses were reburied at municipal cemeteries. The photo shows a temporary cemetery at Nollendorfplatz, the center of Berlin's West. The elevated Nollendorfplatz station with its imperial crown-like dome and fountain had become a ruin. The platform lay on the street.

▷ Potsdamer Straße mit unfertiger Potsdamer Brücke, heute Kulturforum, 1945 weithin zerstörtes Terrain. Oberhalb der Brücke, am jetzigen Standort der Neuen Nationalgalerie, ist der von den Nationalsozialisten geplante »Runde Platz« mit dem Rohbau des »Hauses des Deutschen Fremdenverkehrs« zu sehen. Links davon ein See, der sich in der Baugrube gebildet hatte und den nach Kriegsende Jugendliche als Badestelle und Tanzort nutzten. Diesen Ort zeigt auch das Foto auf dem Umschlag dieses Buches.

▷ *Potsdamer Strasse with the unfinished Potsdamer Bridge, today's Culture Forum, is a vastly destroyed terrain in 1945. Above the bridge, where the New National Gallery stands today, the "Round Plaza" with the unfinished "House of German Tourism," planned by the National Socialists and designed by the architects Theo Dierksmeyer and Hugo Röttcher, can be seen. To the left young people swim and dance at a waterhole formed in the building pit. This watherhole can be seen on the coverphoto.*

1945

20. Juli 1945

20. Juli 1945

20. Juli 1945

20. Juli 1945

Im Juni / Juli 1945 kam aus den Gebieten jenseits der im Potsdamer Abkommen festgelegten Ostgrenze ein riesiger Flüchtlingsstrom in die zerstörte Stadt. Bereits im März hatte die Sowjetunion die deutschen Länder östlich der Oder-Neiße-Linie an Polen übergeben. Die Flüchtlinge durften nur einen Tag in Berlin bleiben und erhielten eine Suppe und 100 Gramm Brot. Wegen Versorgungsengpässen wurde im Juli die Aufnahme weiterer Menschen gestoppt. 537 000 Flüchtlinge wurden nach Brandenburg, Mecklenburg und Sachsen verschickt.

In June / July 1945 a mass of refugees from the territories east of the border set by the Potsdam Agreement poured into the destroyed city. By March the Soviet Union had already handed over to Poland the German states east of the Oder-Neisse line. The refugees were only permitted to stay in Berlin for one day and were given a soup and 100 grams of bread. The flow of refugees entering the city was stopped in July due to a shortage of food. 537,000 refugees were redirected to Brandenburg, Mecklenburg und Saxony.

▷ Während in der Joachimsthaler Straße, vor dem Bahnhof Zoologischer Garten, im Herbst 1945 bereits wieder eine provisorische Straßenbahnhaltestelle eingerichtet war (oben), blieb das Regierungsviertel noch für Jahre eine Trümmerlandschaft (unten). Der Blick geht von den Ruinen an der Wilhelmstraße über den Pariser Platz mit dem Brandenburger Tor zum Reichstagsgebäude, das noch seine ursprüngliche Kuppel besitzt. Diese wurde 1954 gesprengt und 1994–99 im Zuge des Reichstagsumbaus durch eine reine Glaskonstruktion ersetzt.

▷ *A temporary streetcar stop was re-established in front of the Zoological Gardens station on Joachimsthaler Strasse by the fall of 1945 (above), but the government quarter remained an expanse of rubble for many years (below). The view runs from the ruins on Wilhelmstrasse across the Pariser Platz and Brandenburg Gate to the Reichstag building with its original cupola. This cupola was demolished in 1954 and replaced with a completely new glass dome during renovations of the Reichstag in 1994–99.*

4. Oktober 1945

um 1948

1947

1945

Die gesamte Berliner Innenstadt war eine Ruinenlandschaft. Von der ab 1260 errichteten frühgotischen Klosterkirche standen nur noch die Westfront, die Nordmauer und der Chor. Im Hintergrund ist der während der Endkämpfe beschädigte Turm des Rathauses zu erkennen. – Auch die Tauentzienstraße bot ein trauriges Bild. Die Straßenbahngleise sind zerstört, der Tunnel der Untergrundbahn ist geöffnet, das Wahrzeichen des Berliner Westens, die Kaiser-Wilhelm-Gedächtniskirche, ist schwer beschädigt.

▷ Besonders schwer hatten es in der unmittelbaren Nachkriegszeit die alten Menschen. Sie, die teilweise bereits den Ersten Weltkrieg miterlebt hatten, litten besonders unter der schlechten Versorgung mit Lebensmitteln und dem Mangel an Unterkünften. Die Altersheime waren dramatisch überbelegt. – In den Notjahren gehörte der Austausch von Waren zum elementaren Alltagsleben. An vielen Berliner Hausruinen wurden Waren zum Tausch angeboten oder Verwandte und Bekannte gesucht.

The entire city center of Berlin stood in ruins. Only the west front, north wall and chancel of the early Gothic cloister church of 1260 still stood after the war. The tower of the city hall, damaged in the final battles around Berlin, is visible in the photo. – Tauentzienstrasse was also a sad sight. The streetcar tracks are destroyed; the tunnel of the underground railway is open; The Kaiser Wilhelm Memorial Church, the landmark of Berlin's West, built in 1891–1895 by Franz Schwechten, is severely damaged.

▷ *The elderly people, many of whom had also lived through the First World War, had a particularly difficult time right after the war ended. They suffered tremendously from the lack of food supplies and the shortage of housing facilities. The homes for the elderly were dramatically overcrowded. – During these difficult years trading goods became a basic part of daily life. People used the ruins of former buildings in Berlin to offer goods for trade and search for lost relatives and friends.*

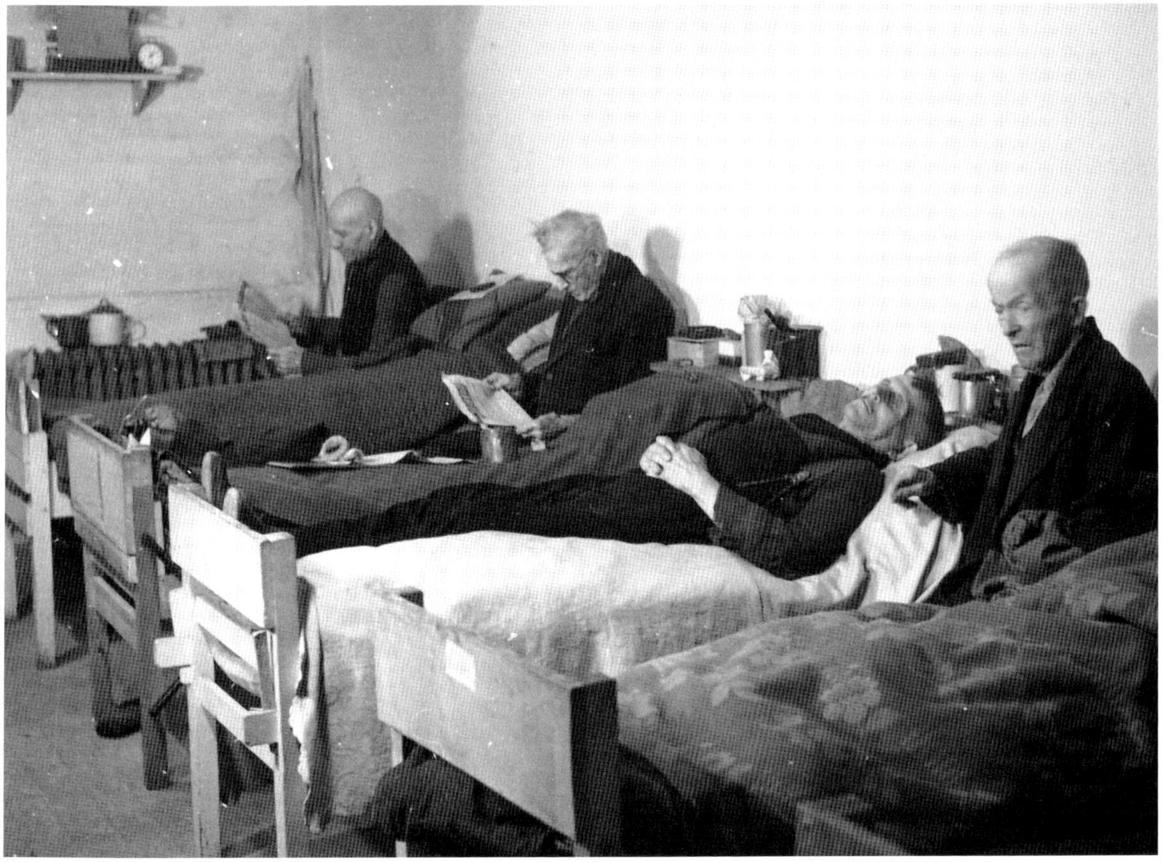

1946

um 1948

21. Juli 1945

Zu den Zeugnissen der unsinnigen, fast zwei Wochen dauernden Straßenkämpfe in Berlin gehörten neben den Einschlägen in Häuserfronten das herrenlos auf den Straßen herumstehende zerstörte Kriegsmaterial. Panzer, wie hier in der Hermannstraße im Bezirk Neukölln, Flakgeschütze oder Panzersperren bildeten für Kinder und Jugendliche eine ideale Spielmöglichkeit. Es waren allenthalben die jungen Menschen, die als Erste inmitten von Not und Zerstörung wieder Lebensfreude entwickelten.

In addition to the many bullet holes on the fronts of buildings, destroyed military equipment lie abandoned on the streets as evidence of the almost two week long nonsensical street fighting in Berlin during the last days of the war. Tanks, like this one on Hermannstrasse in the Neukölln district, anti-aircraft artillery and anti-tank obstacles provided children with ideal material to play with. Young people were the first to rediscover a zest for life amidst the deprivation and destruction.

▷ Auch in den Grünanlagen war zerstörtes Kriegsmaterial anzufinden. Das Foto zeigt eine Flugzeugabwehrkanone, kurz Flak genannt, im Tiergarten, nahe des Großen Sterns mit der Siegessäule. – Ruinen in der Mitte der Berliner Altstadt: an der Friedrichsgracht zwischen Grünstraßenbrücke, ganz links, und Gertraudenbrücke. Hinter den Ruinen, in der Mitte des Fotos, liegt der Spittelmarkt. Ab 1971 entstanden an der Stelle der zerstörten Bauten auf der rechten Seite die Neubauten der Fischerinsel.

▷ *War material could also be found strewn about in parks. This photo shows an anti-aircraft gun, called flak in shortform, in the Tiergarten near the Grosse Stern traffic circle and Victory Column. – Ruins in the center of Berlin's old city: on the Friedrich Canal between the Grünstrasse Bridge, to the far left, and Gertrauden Bridge. The Spittelmarkt lies behind the ruins in the center of the photo. The destroyed buildings on the right were replaced with the new Fischerinsel buildings in 1971.*

Februar 1945

um 1946

um 1947

Verzweifelt versuchen Frauen, von einem Baum im Großen Tiergarten Brennholz abzutrennen. In den kalten Wintern 1945 / 1946 sowie 1946 / 1947 litten die Berliner dramatisch unter dem Mangel an Brennmaterial und behalfen sich, indem sie einfach die Grünanlagen abholzten. Das abgeholzte Gelände wurde den Anwohnern, nach einem Beschluss des Magistrats vom 25.4.1946, als Grabeland zur Verfügung gestellt. Auf den etwa 2500 Parzellen wurden pro Jahr etwa 20 Tonnen Gemüse und Kartoffeln geerntet.

In desperation, women try to break off branches from a tree in the Grosser Tiergarten. In the cold winter of 1945 / 1946 and 1946 / 1947 Berliners suffered greatly from the lack of firewood and took to cutting down trees in parks for kindling. The local authorities passed a resolution on April 25, 1946 which made the cleared out grounds available to the population as garden plots. Each year approximately twenty tons of vegetables and potatoes were planted on the ca. 2500 parcels of land.

▷ Die ganze Not der Nachkriegszeit spricht aus diesem Foto. Eine Frau zieht ihren mit Brennholz beladenen Wagen gen Osten, in Richtung Brandenburger Tor. Sie hat das Holz im Großen Tiergarten geschlagen. In wenigen Tagen wird sie es verbraucht haben und erneut Brennmaterial organisieren müssen. Durch das widerrechtliche Abholzen der Bäume entstanden den Parkanlagen schwere Schäden. Von den rund 200 000 Bäumen im Tiergarten blieben nur etwa 700 stehen, die auch noch teilweise an den Splittern in den Stämmen erkrankten.

▷ *The photo conveys many of the difficulties of the postwar period. A woman pulls her wagon full of firewood eastward toward the Brandenburg Gate. She cut the wood down from trees in the Grosse Tiergarten. She will have used it all up within a couple of days and begin looking for new material to burn. The park grounds suffered great damage from the illegal felling of trees. Of the 200,000 or so trees in the Tiergarten, only about 700 remained, many of which became diseased from shell splinters in their trunks.*

Winter 1945 / 1946

1947

Der Lützowplatz, einst einer der schönsten Stadtplätze Berlins, wurde vor allen Dingen während der Endkämpfe zerstört. Den Platz, der Zentrum des Kunst- und Antiquitätenhandels war, betonte und zierte eine 1903 eingeweihte Brunnenanlage des Bildhauers Otto Lessing. Sie stellte Herkules als Befreier des Prometheus dar, der den Menschen das Feuer vom Himmel brachte und deshalb von den neidischen Göttern an den Felsen geschmiedet wurde. Das den Platz umgebende Lützow-Viertel zählte zu den bevorzugten Wohngegenden der Stadt.

▷ Das historische Zentrum: ein riesiges Ruinenfeld. Auf der Brüderstraße, einst eine urbane Straße mit Geschäften und Kneipen, steht ein kleines Mädchen vor Ruinen, wie auf einem Erinnerungsfoto. An der zur Schlossfreiheit führenden Straße entstand zwischen 1962 und 1964 das SED-Staatsratsgebäude. – Ruinenstille auch auf der Kurstraße, die den Werderschen Markt mit dem Spittelmarkt verbindet. Heute steht hier das Auswärtige Amt, bestehend aus dem ehemaligen Reichsbankgebäude von 1934-1940 und einem Anbau von 1999.

The Lützowplatz, once one of the loveliest plazas in Berlin, suffered terrible damage during the final battles. A 1903 fountain by the sculptor Otto Lessing accentuates and adorns the plaza, which had once been the center of the arts and antique business. It depicts Hercules as the liberator of Prometheus, who was chained to a rock by the jealous gods after he gave man fire from heaven. The Lützow Quarter around the plaza had been one of the most desirable residential neighborhoods in the city.

▷ *The historic center is a huge sea of ruins. As if posing for a snapshot, a little girl stands in front of the ruins on Brüderstrasse, once an urban street with stores and bars. The SED council of state building was erected between 1962 and 1964 on the street leading to the Schlossfreiheit plaza. – Quiet ruins on Kurstrasse, which connects the Werdersche Markt with the Spittelmarkt. Today the Foreign Office stands here, consisting of the former Reich Bank building of 1934-1940 and the extension added in 1999.*

1947

1946/1947

Mai 1945

Als der Rauch der gänzlich überflüssigen Endkämpfe um die Hauptstadt noch nicht richtig verflogen war, ordnete der am 28.4.1945 zum sowjetischen Stadtkommandanten ernannte Generaloberst Bersarin die Bildung des Magistrats als oberstes Verwaltungsorgan von Groß-Berlin an. Ihm ist es zu verdanken, dass bereits vor dem Ende der Kampfhandlungen die Aufräumarbeiten und die Versorgung der Bevölkerung begannen. Die ersten Befehle der Sieger und Befreier wurden in russischer und deutscher Sprache an Litfaßsäulen angebracht.

▷ Ein Erinnerungsfoto vor dem Reichstagsgebäude war ein beliebtes Souvenir für die Soldaten der Roten Armee. Das Gebäude galt nach dem Reichstagsbrand von 1933 und der damit einhergehenden »Machtergreifung« Hitlers als Symbol des deutschen Faschismus. Am 30. April um 20.50 Uhr war es endlich so weit: Die Rote Armee hatte nach schweren Kämpfen, teilweise um einzelne Räume, das Reichstagsgebäude besetzt und die Rote Fahne als Symbol des Sieges über den Nationalsozialismus gehisst.

Before the smoke from the needless final battles around the capital had faded, Senior General Bersarin, appointed Soviet City Commander on April 28, 1945, ordered the establishment of a local authority to serve as the supreme administrative organ of Greater Berlin. It is thanks to him that clean-up work began and the population was given supplies even before the fighting had ceased. The first orders of the victors and liberators were posted on advertisement pillars in both German and Russian.

▷ *A snapshot in front of the Reichstag building was a popular souvenir for the soldiers of the Red Army. Following the Reichstag fire of 1933 and the accompanying "seizure of power" by Hitler and his party, the building became a symbol of German fascism. On April 30, at 8:50 in the evening, the moment finally arrived: Following heavy fighting, in part for individual rooms, the Red Army occupied the Reichstag building and hoisted the Red Flag as a symbol of victory over National Socialism.*

Oktober 1945

1945

Oktober 1945

Zwei Gesichter der Müllerstraße. An der Ecke Seestraße stellte die französische Besatzungsmacht zur Orientierung ihrer Truppen Hinweisschilder auf. Die Franzosen hatten die nördlichen Bezirke Wedding und Reinickendorf von den Briten übernommen. – Am östlichen Ende der Müllerstraße fand sich ein sowjetisches Propagandaschild mit einem Zitat Stalins. Auf der gegenüberliegenden Straßenseite beseitigen Frauen provisorisch den Schutt von den Straßen, während ein Junge barfuß die Straße entlangläuft.

▷ Der Große Stern mit der Siegessäule wurde zum Treffpunkt der Soldaten der vier Besatzungsmächte. Vor dem 1938 vom Königsplatz (Platz der Republik) wegen der Umgestaltung Berlins zur »Welthauptstadt Germania« hierher umgesetzten Bismarck-Denkmal posieren sie für Erinnerungsfotos. Oben links amerikanische, oben rechts französische Soldaten, unten links russische Soldaten und Soldatinnen mit anderen Frauen; unten rechts lassen sich sowjetische Soldaten und britische Soldaten (2. und 4. von links) gemeinsam fotografieren.

The photos show the two contrasting faces of Müllerstrasse: The French occupying forces set up directional signs on the corner of Seestrasse to help their troops find their way around the foreign city. The French took over the northern districts of Wedding and Reinickendorf from the British. – On the eastern end of Müllerstrasse a Soviet propaganda sign displays a quote from Secretary-general Stalin. A young boy walks barefoot down the street while women remove war debris across the street.

▷ *The Grosser Stern and Victory Column became a meeting place for soldiers of all four occupying powers. They pose for snapshots in front of the Bismarck monument, which was moved here in 1938 from Königsplatz (Platz der Republik) as part of the plans to redesign Berlin into the "Germania World Capital." Upper left: American soldiers; upper right: French soldiers; lower left: Russian soldiers, both male and female, with other women; Lower right: Soviet and British soldiers (2nd and 4th from left) have their picture taken together.*

um 1946

um 1946

um 1946

um 1946

3. November 1945

Ein Heimkehrer aus der Kriegsgefangenschaft, abgemagert, mit provisorischen Schuhen, steht an der Spree, am Washington-Platz, in unmittelbarer Nähe des Lehrter Bahnhofes, und sieht hinüber auf die zerstörten Gebäude am Königsplatz (Platz der Republik). Noch 1945 kamen die ersten Berliner Männer aus der Gefangenschaft zurück. Sie fanden sich in einer fremden Welt wieder: Die bekannten Straßenzüge und Häuser waren größtenteils zerstört oder standen als Ruinen; Verwandte und Freunde mussten erst ausfindig gemacht werden.

▷ Die Welt der Kriegsheimkehrer und Flüchtlinge war erschütternd und deprimierend. Zu den Bevorzugten zählten noch diejenigen, die eine Unterkunft besaßen – etwa hier im Kriegsheimkehrer- und Flüchtlingslager in der Ruschestraße in Lichtenberg. Ein Mann mit Krücken, ein anderer mit Kopfverband, über ihre wenigen Habseligkeiten wachend: So sah für viele das Leben nach dem Krieg aus. – Ein Ausgebombter? Ein Flüchtling? Wir wissen es nicht. Doch das Bild zeigt beispielhaft, was der Nationalsozialismus hinterlassen hatte.

A prisoner of war returning home from captivity, emaciated, with makeshift shoes, stands at the Spree River at Washington Platz close to the Lehrter station and looks over at the destroyed buildings at Königsplatz (Platz der Republik). The first men returned to Berlin from captivity as early as 1945. They found themselves in a foreign world: Many streets and buildings were completely destroyed or stood as mere ruins; the search for relatives and friends began. It was especially important for them to remain realistic and focus on the present.

▷ *The world of refugees and people returning from the war was upsetting and depressing. The lucky ones had a place to live – like here in a camp for war returnees and refugees on Ruschestrasse in Lichtenberg. A man on crutches, another with head bandages, guard their few possessions: This is what life was like for so many after the war. – Was the man bombed out of his home, or perhaps a refugee? We don't know. But the photo gives a good impression of what National Socialism left behind.*

Januar 1947

Mai 1945

Mai 1946

Was ist aus dem einst so gloriosen Berliner Westen geworden? Der U-Bahnhof Wittenbergplatz steht als Ruine mitten auf dem gleichnamigen Platz. Er scheint funktionslos geworden zu sein. Die Gleise der Straßenbahn liegen zwar, aber die Oberleitung fehlt. Und wie steht es um das stolze Kaufhaus des Westens (das wir links im Bild sehen)! Auch der ehemalige Konsumtempel, weit über Berlin hinaus bekannt, ist nur noch eine Ruine. Die Wiedereröffnung des KaDeWe fand bereits vier Jahre später statt, im Juli 1950.

▷ Die Bellevuestraße, im Tiergartenviertel gelegen und eine der besten Adressen Berlins; im Hintergrund Potsdamer Platz mit Columbushaus. Das Foto verdeutlicht das Drama der Zeit: Flüchtlinge ziehen mit ihren geringen Habseligkeiten in die Berliner Innenstadt – nicht ahnend, dass sie hier nicht bleiben dürfen. – Am Gendarmenmarkt war die Welt des lebensbejahenden Barocks verklungen. Die Kirchen und das Schauspielhaus waren ausgebrannt oder durch Bomben zerstört, der Endkampf um Berlin hatte sein Übriges getan.

What became of the once so glorious Berlin West? The Wittenbergplatz subway station stands in ruins at the center of the plaza of the same name. It appears to have lost its function. The streetcar tracks are still intact, but the overhead cables are missing. And what about the proud Kaufhaus des Westens department store on the left? Even this former temple of consumption, famous well beyond the borders of Berlin, is a mere ruin. The KaDeWe department store opened its doors again in July 1950.

▷ *The Bellevue Strasse, one of the best locations in Berlin, lies in the Tiergarten quarter; Potsdamer Platz with Columbushaus is visible in the background. The photo depicts the dramatic times: Refugees move with their few possessions to the Berlin city center – not knowing that they won't be allowed to stay here. – At Gendarmenmarkt the world of life-affirming Baroque is gone. The two churches and Schauspielhaus theater were burned out or destroyed by bombs. The final battles around Berlin took care of the rest.*

um 1946

1948

um 1946

Die ungenügende Versorgung der Bevölkerung bescherte in der Nachkriegszeit dem Schwarzen Markt, dem illegalen Handel mit Waren, die wegen ihrer Knappheit legal nur auf Bezugsschein zu erhalten waren, einen Aufschwung unerhörten Ausmaßes. Die Preise auf dem Schwarzen Markt betrugen oft das 30fache der amtlich festgesetzten Preise. Das Foto zeigt Schwarzhändler und ihre Kunden am Nationaldenkmal Kaiser Wilhelm I. (das 1950 abgetragen und eingeschmolzen wurde) an der Schlossfreiheit.

The insufficient supply of goods for the population in the postwar period led to the establishment of a booming black market, the illegal trade of goods, which because of their scarcity were only available with ration coupons. The prices of the black market were often thirty times higher than official prices. The photo shows black marketers and their customers at the Kaiser Wilhelm I national monument (that was removed and melted down in 1950) on the Schlossfreiheit plaza close to the City Palace.

▷ Schwarze Märkte gab es in Berlin an mehreren Stellen. Hier sehen wir, wie sowjetische Soldaten auf dem Potsdamer Platz verhandeln. Im Hintergrund Columbushaus (rechts) und Pschorrhaus. – Um den Schwarzhandel zu unterbinden, führte die Polizei immer wieder Razzien durch, wie hier am Reichstagsgebäude (links). Das Schnellgericht des Bezirks Mitte sah sich 1947 allerdings außerstande, Personen zu verurteilen, die aus einer bitteren Notlage heraus persönliche Gegenstände des täglichen Lebens verkauft hatten.

▷ *Black markets emerged at many different places in Berlin in the years following the war. Here we see Soviet soldiers bargaining on Potsdamer Platz. In the background Columbushaus (right) and Pschorrhaus can be seen. – To stop the black market, police carried out repeated raids, pictured here at the Reichstag building (left). In 1947 the summary court of the Mitte district found itself unable to convict people who were forced to sell their personal possessions out of bitter deprivation.*

um 1948

März 1946

12. November 1952

1948

Das Elend war im Berlin der Nachkriegsjahre überall gegenwärtig – ob in diesem zum provisorischen Wohnraum hergerichteten ehemaligen Kohlenladen in der Willdenowstraße im Bezirk Wedding, in der neun Personen leben mussten (links), oder unterhalb der Siegessäule am Großen Stern, wo Kartoffeln angepflanzt wurden (rechts). Um die prekäre Versorgungslage der Bevölkerung etwas zu mildern, hatte der Berliner Magistrat Grünflächen und Parkanlagen in Äcker oder Gärten umwandeln lassen.

▷ Besonders stark waren durch die schlechte Versorgung mit Lebensmitteln die Kinder betroffen. Man versuchte, in den Melkereien der Stadt wenigstens Milch für die Kleinkinder zu erhalten. In langen Warteschlangen stand man auf den Höfen vor der Milchausgabe. – Wenn es sich herumsprach, dass es irgendwo Lebensmittel zu kaufen gab, kamen die Berliner sofort in Scharen. Hier wird der Verkauf von Kartoffeln, die einfach auf die Straße geschüttet wurden, von einem Polizisten überwacht.

The widespread misery in Berlin during the postwar years was everywhere, for example in this coal store on Willdenowstrasse in Wedding, which was converted into a temporary living room for nine people (left), or below the Victory Column at the Grosse Stern traffic circle, where potatoes were grown (right). To help compensate for the precarious supply of goods available to the population, Berlin municipal authorities allowed green areas and parks to be converted into fields and gardens.

▷ *The lack of food available to the population was especially detrimental to the children of the war. Parents and grandparents went to the city's dairies in the hope of getting at least enough milk for their small children. They waited in long lines in the courtyards where milk was distributed. – Whenever word got out that food was for sale somewhere in the city, Berliners arrived in droves. In this picture a policemen is guarding the sale of potatoes that have simply been dumped onto the street.*

1945

Juni 1945

um 1945

17. Oktober 1949

In der Berliner Innenstadt warten Menschen an einer Haltestelle der Straßenbahn. Nur einer kann sitzen – auf seinem glücklich erworbenen Gut, das er tunlichst nicht ohne Aufsicht lässt. – Auch nicht bequemer sitzt es sich auf dieser Bank an der Ecke Levetzowstraße / Gotzkowskystraße. Das Holz der Sitzfläche und der Rückenlehne wurde im Winter 1945 / 1946 verheizt. Da es neue Brillengläser nicht gab, behilft sich dieser Mann damit, dass er ein Vergrößerungsglas zwischen Brille und Buch hält.

People wait at a streetcar stop in the center of Berlin. Only one person was lucky enough to find a place to sit – and is doing his very best to hold on to his good fortune. – The bench at the corner of Levetzowstrasse / Gotzkowskystrasse doesn't provide much more comfort. The wood from the seat and armrests was presumably burned for heat in the winter of 1945 / 1946. Since new reading glasses are not available, this man is holding a magnifying glass between his glasses and the book.

▷ So sah es an einem der einst verkehrsreichsten Plätze in Europa aus. Die Umbauung des Potsdamer Platzes mit seinen Bierhäusern und Hotels war zerstört. Die Einmündung der Bellevuestraße wird flankiert von Weinhaus Rheingold und Hotel Esplanade (links) sowie Columbushaus (rechts). – Am 25.5.1945 hatte der Militärkommandant der Stadt Berlin, Generaloberst Bersarin, den Deutschen erlaubt, die Stadtpolizei, das Gerichtswesen und die Staatsanwaltschaft zu organisieren. Hier wird der Fahrer eines Pferdefuhrwerkes kontrolliert.

▷ *This is what it looked like at one of the once busiest plazas in Europe: The Potsdamer Platz with its pre-war beer houses and hotels was destroyed. The intersection of Bellevuestrasse is flanked by Weinhaus Rheingold and Hotel Esplanade (left) and Columbushaus (right). – On May 25, 1945, Senior General Bersarin, military commander of Berlin, permitted Germans to establish a city police, court system and prosecuting attorneys office. Here the driver of the horse and cart is being checked by police.*

April 1946

September 1946

März 1945

1948

August 1946

August 1946

Beispielhaft zeigen diese Bilder die Not der Bevölkerung unmittelbar nach dem Krieg: Notspeisung im »Haus Vaterland« an der Stresemannstraße unweit des Potsdamer Platzes, einst eine der beliebtesten Vergnügungsstätten Berlins (oben links); behelfsmäßige Trinkwasserversorgung wegen vieler im Endkampf zerstörter Hauptrohre (oben rechts); notdürftig mit Restmaterialien geflickte Kinderschuhe, schnell zerschlissen beim Spielen in den Ruinen (unten links); Anstehen nach Lebensmitteln (unten rechts).

▷ Auch diese Fotografie aus dem Frühjahr 1949 dokumentiert eindrucksvoll die Dramatik der Versorgung der Bevölkerung, besonders der älteren Menschen, mit Nahrungsmitteln. Der Notstand machte es nötig, dass das Internationale Komitee des Roten Kreuzes noch vier Jahre nach Beendigung des Krieges eine Winternotspeisung, eine Altenspeisung organisierte. Über Mittag konnten sich hier hilfsbedürftige alte Frauen und Männer mit Kochgeschirren oder Töpfen warmes Mittagessen abholen.

These pictures also reflect the hardship endured by the population. Food for the needy in Haus Vaterland on Stresemannstrasse, just off of Potsdamer Platz, once one of the most popular entertainment locations in Berlin (above left); a supplemental water supply, necessary because so many main pipes were destroyed during the last battles (above right); Children's shoes, crudely patched up with left over material, tear quickly during play in the ruins (below left); long lines for food (below right).

▷ *These photographs taken in the spring of 1949 give a good impression of the difficulties involved in supplying food to the population, especially the elderly. The extreme conditions made it necessary for the International Committee of the Red Cross to prepare a warm meal in winter for the needy and elderly for four years after the war. At lunchtime old people who were unable to provide for themselves could bring their own cooking utensils or pots here and pick up a warm meal.*

Winternotspeisung
Essenausgabe
12 - 14 Uhr
ALTENSPEISUNG
INTERNATIONALE KOMITEE VOM ROTEN KREUZ

April 1949

1946

1946 / 1947

Juni 1945

1947

Wie erstarrt lag die Innenstadt da: Friedrichswerdersche Kirche und Bauakademie (oben links); die Budapester Straße, einst Flanierstraße zum Tiergarten, mit den Ruinen der Zoo-Festsäle, an deren Stelle seit 1958 das Hotel »Berlin Hilton« steht (oben rechts); Blick von der Ecke Mauerstraße / Kronenstraße auf das »Kleisthaus« und einen Ruinenberg, den die 1943 durch Bomben zerstörte Dreifaltigkeitskirche und ein Bunker für die Gauleitung der NSDAP hinterließ (unten links); Reichpietschufer mit Potsdamer Brücke (unten rechts).

▷ Das 1695–1699 erbaute, mehrmals erweiterte Charlottenburger Schloss wurde bei dem Luftangriff vom 22.11.1943 zerstört. Die bei dem Brand eingestürzte Kuppel wurde 1956 / 57 in alter Form rekonstruiert. Ab August 1950 waren einige der wiederhergestellten Räume für die Öffentlichkeit wieder zu besichtigen. – Weniger stark zerstört und dennoch 1950 gesprengt, um Platz für die Demonstrationen der DDR zu schaffen: das ab 1699 zur Barockresidenz umgebaute Stadtschloss in der Mitte Berlins. Im Bild das Portal III mit der Kuppel.

The city center appears frozen in time: The Friedrichswerder Church and Building Academy (above left); the Budapester Strasse, once created a promenade to the Tiergarten, with the ruins of the zoo banquet hall. The Berlin Hilton was built there in 1958 (above right); view from the corner of Mauerstrasse / Kronenstrasse of the Kleisthaus and a mountain of ruins left behind by the Trinity Church and a NSDAP Gau leadership bunker after they were destroyed by a bomb in 1943 (below left); Reichpietschufer with Potsdamer Bridge (below right).

▷ *The Charlottenburg Palace, built in 1695-1699 and expanded on numerous occasions, was heavily damaged by an air raid on November 22, 1943. The dome, which collapsed during a fire, was rebuilt in its original form from 1956 to 1957. By August 1950 some of the reconstructed rooms were once again open to public view. – The City Palace in the middle of Berlin, converted in 1699 into a baroque residence, was less severely damaged, but nonetheless torn down in 1950. The picture shows the Portal III with the cupola.*

um 1946

um 1946

19. April 1949

Noch vier Jahre nach Ende der Kampfhandlungen standen auf manchen Berliner Straßen und Plätzen zerstörte Fahrzeuge der deutschen Wehrmacht herum. Für Kinder, weiblichen wie männlichen Geschlechts gleichermaßen, bildeten die Hinterlassenschaften des Krieges ideale Abenteuerspielplätze, wie man an diesem Beispiel aus der Eisackstraße im Bezirk Schöneberg gut erkennen kann. Das beliebte Werfen mit noch nicht beseitigten Trümmersteinen endete allerdings teilweise mit blutenden Wunden.

Four years after the fighting had stopped, destroyed German military vehicles still stood strewn about on a number of streets and places in Berlin. For children, both boys and girls, the remains of the war provided lots to discover and ideal areas for running, playing and having adventures. A good example is seen here on the Eisackstrasse in the Schöneberg district. But throwing about the left behind stones and rubble, which was popular those days, sometimes led to unfortunate bloody injuries.

▷ Die Enttrümmerung der großteils zerstörten Innenstadt prägte die ersten Nachkriegsjahre: In die Ruine der Dreifaltigkeitskirche werden Sprenglöcher gebohrt (oben links); Mitarbeiter des Deutschen Theaters helfen beim Enttrümmern (oben rechts); in der Hagelberger Straße in Kreuzberg tragen Frauen eimerweise den Schutt ab, den die Männer verursacht haben (unten links); Frauen beim »Steineklopfen« (unten rechts). Den Trümmerfrauen ist ihre Arbeit nie gedankt worden, dabei schufen gerade sie die Grundlage für den Wiederaufbau.

▷ *During the first years Berliners were busy removing debris from the totally destroyed city center: Blast holes are drilled into the ruins of the Trinity Church (above left); Employees of the Deutsche Theater help remove the rubble (above right); on Hagelberger Strasse in Kreuzberg women carry away buckets of rubble created by the men (below left); women "knocking stones" (below right). The women who cleared away the rubble were never thanked for their hard work, although they established the groundwork for the reconstruction.*

Juni 1945

um 1948

19. April 1949

1946

1947

Im Bezirk Charlottenburg, der zum Britischen Sektor gehörte, stellten die Engländer Lastkraftwagen der Armee zum Abtransport der Trümmer zur Verfügung, wie hier in der Wallstraße, die am 31.7.1947 in Zillestraße umbenannt wurde. Interessant an diesem Foto ist nicht zuletzt, dass hier keine Frauen mehr bei der Enttrümmerung helfen. Dafür hat das junge Mädchen vorn im Bild wahrscheinlich für den Nachschub des Bieres gesorgt, das den Trümmermännern die Arbeit schmackhaft machen soll.

In the district of Charlottenburg, which was part of the British sector, the English provided military trucks to cart off the rubble, as seen here on Wallstrasse, renamed Zillestrasse on July 1, 1947. This photo is also interesting because it shows that the women are no longer involved in clearing away the rubble and debris. But this young girl probably did provide another round of beer to the men who clear away the rubble in an attempt to make the work a little more pleasant for them.

▷ Besonders stark zerstört waren die Wohnhäuser an der Frankfurter Allee. Nach Beendigung der ersten Aufräumarbeiten sind die von Putz und Mörtel befreiten Ziegelsteine fein säuberlich aufgestapelt. Eine Trümmerbahn fährt weiteren Trümmerschutt aus der Straße. – Die Trümmerbahnen fuhren den Schutt zu Sammeldepots. Dieses Zwischenlager befand sich an der Burgstraße. Im Hintergrund der Dom mit provisorisch abgedeckter Kuppel und die 1975 / 76 abgebrochene Denkmalskirche, davor die Sandsteinobelisken der Friedrichsbrücke.

▷ *The residential buildings on Frankfurter Allee were especially badly damaged. After the first phase of clearing work was complete, the bricks, cleaned of any concrete and mortar, are neatly stacked. A rubble rail carries more rubble and debris away from the street. – The rubble rail carries the debris to collection depots. This provisional site was located on Burgstrasse. In the background the cathedral is shown with a temporarily covered dome and the memorial church, torn down in 1976/76; In front of it stands the obelisk of the Friedrich Bridge.*

April 1946

18. Juni 1949

12. Oktober 1953

Um die ungeheuren Trümmermassen, die der Krieg hinterlassen hatte, wieder zu gebrauchsfähigen Baumaterialien umzuwandeln, entstanden Ziegelbrechwerke, in denen die Trümmersteine zermahlen wurden. Es entstand Ziegelmehl, aus dem dann unter dem Zusatz von Ton Hohlblocksteine gebrannt wurden. Hier sehen wir auf die Trümmerverwertungsanlage an der Jebensstraße in unmittelbarer Nähe des Bahnhofs Zoologischer Garten. Bizarr recken sich die ruinösen Türme der Kaiser-Wilhelm-Gedächtniskirche in den Herbsthimmel.

▷ 1948 kam es zu Spannungen zwischen den westlichen Alliierten und der sowjetischen Besatzungsmacht. Um die Wirtschaftskraft zu stabilisieren, führten die drei Westalliierten in ihren westdeutschen Zonen eine neue Währung ein. Am 24.6.1948 wurde die Westmark, wie sie genannt wurde, auch in den Westsektoren Berlins eingeführt. Im Zusammenhang mit der Währungsreform standen die von der SED organisierten massiven Störungen der Stadtverordnetenversammlung vor dem Neuen Stadthaus, die das Foto zeigt.

To convert the large amounts of rubble left behind by the war into usable building material, a number of brick crushing plants were established to grind the debris. Brick powder was then created which when added to clay could be burned into hollow blocks. In this photo we see the rubble recycling facilities located on Jebensstrasse, right next to the Zoologischer Garten railway station. The broken towers of the Kaiser Wilhelm Memorial Church stretch bizarrely into the autumn sky.

▷ *In 1948 conflicts developed between the Western Allies and the Soviet occupying powers. To stabilize the economic crisis the Western Allies introduced a new currency into their West German zones. On June 24, 1948, the West Mark, as it was called, was also introduced into the west sectors of Berlin. In reaction to the currency reform, the East German government organized a demonstration in front of the Neue Stadthaus (seen in photo), organized by the East German government to disrupt the city council assembly.*

Magistrat
von Groß Berlin
Hauptverwaltung
Neues Stadthaus
Magistrat
von Groß Berlin
Hauptverwaltung
Neues Stadthaus

23. Juni 1948

September 1948

Nach der Wiederaufnahme des Schulunterrichts am 11.6.1945 führte Otto Winzer, der im Mai 1945 die Leitung des Berliner Volksbildungswesen übernommen hatte und die Neuordnung des Schulwesens im Sinne eines deutschen Weges zum Sozialismus anstrebte, eine Einheitsschule von der 1. bis zur 10. Klasse ein. Hier sehen wir in einen Klassenraum der 2. Schule Reinickendorf in der Waldstraße. Die Tische – teilweise viel zu niedrig – und die Sitzgelegenheiten sind notdürftig zusammengesucht.

After the schools re-opened on June 11, 1945, Otto Winzer, who was appointed director of the Berlin elementary school system in May 1945 and who strove to restructure the school education system according to the German path to Socialism, introduced a uniform school for the first to the tenth grades. Here we are looking into a classroom of the Second School Reinickendorf on Waldstrasse. The classroom tables, many of them much too low, and the chairs have been hastily gathered together.

▷ Not macht erfinderisch. Manch einer legte in einem Trümmerfeld einen provisorischen Garten an. Das Foto zeigt das Ruinengrundstück Ecke Levetzowstraße / Zinzendorfstraße. Eine Umzäunung aus Ziegelsteinen, Eisenträgern und Ruinenschrott soll Diebe abhalten. Links steht noch ein Verteidigungsstand aus Beton. – Hamsterfahrten führten viele Menschen aus Berlin in die Umgebung, wo sie auf Bauernhöfen Kartoffeln, Korn oder Obst eintauschten. Der überfüllte Zug fährt durch den Bahnhof Wildpark in Potsdam.

▷ *Necessity breeds creativity. Some people planted a garden on a field of rubble. The photo shows a plot of ruins at the corner of Levetzowstrasse / Zinzendorfstrasse. A barrier of bricks, iron girders and junk from the ruins is designed to keep thieves away. A defense structure made of concrete still stands on the left. – Many people embarked on foraging trips to farms on the outskirts of Berlin to exchange goods for potatoes, grain or fruit. The crowded train is running through the Wildpark station in Potsdam.*

1948

1946

um 1946

Das Leben geht weiter, die Schrecken des Kriegs geraten in Vergessenheit … Im Vordergrund deutet ein Kreuz aus Birkenstämmen und Stahlhelmen an, dass die Kämpfe auch diese idyllische Landschaft an der Havel nicht verschont haben. Gleich neben dem Grab tönt aus einem transportablen Grammophon Musik. Man sonnt sich, badet, zeigt die Bademoden der Zeit, und auf dem Wasser fahren schon wieder Boote. Ganz normales Badeleben also – bis auf die Soldatengräber im Strandsand.

Life goes on and the horror of the war falls into oblivion … In the foreground a cross made of birch branches and steel helmets suggests that not even this idyllic landscape on the Havel River was spared during the insane fighting. Right next to the grave, music plays from a portable gramophone. People sunbathe and swim, displaying the newest swimwear fashions, and boats ride on the water once again. Normal beach life – were it not for the soldier graves buried in the sand.

▷ Als Folge der Währungsreform sperrte die sowjetische Militäradministration die Zufahrtswege nach West-Berlin. Nach dem Beginn der Sperrmaßnahmen ordnete der Militärgouverneur der Amerikanischen Besatzungszone, General Lucius D. Clay, am 25.6.1948 die Versorgung der Westsektoren durch eine Luftbrücke an. Die Berliner fuhren nun nach Tempelhof, dem Hauptlande- und -startplatz der Flugzeuge, um sich die zweimotorigen »Dakotas« oder viermotorigen »Skymaster« anzusehen, die die Güter nach Berlin einflogen.

▷ *In response to the currency reform the Soviet military administration blocked all access routes to West Berlin. After the first blocking measures were taken, General Lucius D. Clay, military governor of the American Zone of Occupation, issued an order on June 25, 1948 for an airlift to provide provisions to the west sectors. The Berliners drove to Tempelhof, the main airplane take-off and landing site, to see the two-motor "Dakotas" and four-motor "Skymasters," which flew the goods into Berlin.*

1948

1948

Der Minimalbedarf West-Berlins betrug rund 5000 Tonnen täglich. Die Transportkapazität der Luftbrücke betrug aber anfangs nur 500 bis 700 Tonnen. Erst die Zusammenlegung der Luftbrücken der Briten und der Amerikaner am 20.10.1948 führte zu der gewünschten Leistungssteigerung. An Flugplätzen standen zunächst nur Tempelhof (im Bild) und Gatow zur Verfügung. Tempelhof erhielt im September, Gatow im April 1949 eine zweite Rollbahn. Nach nur drei Monaten Bauzeit wurde am 5.11.1948 der Flughafen Tegel in Betrieb genommen.

▷ Die Blockade endete am 12.5.1949. Die Luftbrücke wurde allerdings im vollen Umfang bis zum 1.8.1949 fortgesetzt und dann schrittweise bis zum 30.9.1949 eingestellt. Insgesamt wurden in den 462 Tagen der Luftbrücke 1 831 200 Tonnen Güter verschiedenster Art nach West-Berlin geflogen. Das Foto zeigt die Entladung einer amerikanischen Maschine. – Die britische Schutzmacht nutzte neben dem Flugplatz Gatow auch die Havel als Landeplatz. Das erste Sunderland-Flugboot wasserte am 6.7.1948 vor der Entladungsrampe in Kladow.

To cover the needs of West Berlin 5000 tons of supplies were required daily. In the beginning the airlift was only able to transport a maximum of 500 to 700 tons. Not until the British and Americans combined their airlifts on October 20, 1948 was it possible to achieve the desired capacity. At first only the Tempelhof (in photo) and Gatow airfields were available. Tempelhof received a second runway in September; Gatow had one by April 1949. The Tegel airport began operating on November 5, 1948, after only three months of construction.

▷ *The blockade ended on May 12, 1949, but the airlift continued to full capacity until August 1, 1949 and only came to a gradual end by September 30, 1949. During the 462 days of the airlift a total of 1,831,200 tons of goods were flown into Berlin. The photo shows an American plane being unloaded. – In addition to the Gatow airfield, the British protective power also used the Havel River as a landing site. The first Sunderland airboat touched down on water on July 6, 1948 in front of the loading ramp in Kladow.*

August 1948

1948

8. Juni 1954

Kinder spielen in einer Regenpfütze. Sie haben sich Schiffchen aus Papier gefaltet. Barfuss genießen sie die kleinen Wonnen des Sommers. Doch auch diese Szene, an Thaters Privatweg in Plötzensee, ist noch bestimmt vom vergangenen Krieg. Die spielenden Kinder stehen im Kontrast zur realen Brutalität der Betonbauten auf der linken Seite. Sie wurden 1942 als Unterkunftshäuser für die Kraftfahrer des Baustabes Speer gebaut. Die Erdgeschosse wurden von vornherein als Luftschutzbunker angelegt.

Children playing in a puddle of rain. They've folded paper into little boats. Barefoot, they are enjoying the few delights of summer. But even this scene on Thater's private road in Plötzensee is marked by the Second World War. The playing children provide a stark contrast to the brutal reality of the concrete structures on the left side. They were built in 1942 as housing for the truck drivers of Speer's building staff. The ground level was designed to function as an air raid bunker.

▷ Berlin stand voller Ruinen und riesiger Trümmerhaufen, die einst Wohnhäuser waren. Aus der Not machte man oft eine Tugend. Eine Frau hat einen ruinösen Raum im Erdgeschoss, an dem die Vorder- und Seitenwände fehlen, zur Gartenterrasse umfunktioniert. Gartenmöbel sowie ein Mix aus Nutz- und Zierpflanzen in Töpfen und in einer Stellage geben der Szenerie etwas durchaus Gemütliches. Die Wohnung darüber existiert nicht mehr. Den Dachboden des Hauses sichern provisorisch ein paar Holzbalken.

▷ *Berlin was full of ruins and huge piles of debris from what had once been residential apartment buildings. People were often forced to make a virtue out of necessity. A woman turned a damaged room on the ground floor that was missing its front and side walls into a garden patio. Garden furniture and the mixture of useful and ornamental plants in pots and on shelves make it look rather cozy. The apartment above was completely destroyed and no longer exists. A few wooden beams temporarily secure the attic.*

um 1946

1956

Im Krieg war in Berlin jede zweite Wohnung zerstört worden. Um die Wohnungsnot etwas zu lindern, stellten die Briten den deutschen Behörden 1947 sogenannte Nissenhütten zur Verfügung. Eine dieser Nissenhütten-Siedlungen stand an der Halenseestraße in Charlottenburg. Die Hütten verfügten über elektrisches Licht, einen Wasseranschluss und Kanalisation. Der Innenraum war unterteilt in eine Wohnküche, ein Eltern- und ein Kinderschlafzimmer. In der Mitte des Hauses stand ein gemauerter Ofen, der sämtliche Räume heizte.

▷ Alltag im Nachkriegsberlin: Zeitungen und ein Leuchtband, mit dem die »Freie Berliner Presse« Nachrichten in den Ostteil der Stadt sandte, vermelden im Westteil des Potsdamer Platzes den Tod Stalins (oben links); eine Frau bietet in der Badstraße im Bezirk Wedding Kleinwaren zum Verkauf an (oben rechts); der Berliner Magistrat wirbt für die Gleichberechtigung der Frauen im Arbeitsleben (unten links); eine modisch gekleidete Dame lässt ihren kleinen Hund für zehn Pfennige wiegen (unten rechts).

Half the apartments in Berlin were destroyed in the war. In 1947 to alleviate the housing shortage, the British provided the German authorities with residential structures, called Nissen huts. One of these Nissen hut settlements was located on Halenseestrasse in Charlottenburg. They had electric lighting, running water and sewerage. The interiors were divided into a breakfast kitchen, a parents' bedroom and a children's bedroom. A walled in oven stood in the middle of the building providing heat to all the rooms.

▷ *Routine in postwar Berlin: Newspapers and an illuminated display used by the Freie Berliner Presse to send news to the eastern section of the city announces Stalin's death on the west side of Potsdamer Platz (above left); a woman sells small goods in a carrying box on the Badstrasse in the district of Wedding (above right); the Berlin local authorities promote equal rights for working women (below left); a fashionably dressed lady has her dog weighed for ten cents (below right).*

6. März 1953

Februar 1953

November 1946

um 1948

16. Juni 1954

Inmitten von Ruinen begann sich das Leben in den 50er Jahren schnell zu normalisieren. Schon bald vergnügten sich die Berliner wieder auf ihren heißgeliebten Dampferfahrten. Das Foto zeigt einen Ausflugsdampfer auf dem Landwehrkanal, in der Nähe der Potsdamer Brücke. Links ist die Ruine des 1938 erbauten »Haus des Deutschen Fremdenverkehrs« am »Runden Platz« – dem heutigen Standort der Neuen Nationalgalerie – zu erkennen. Dass die Herren Krawatten trugen, gehörte zum guten Ton.

Normal life amidst the war ruins began to set in quickly in the fifties and Berliners soon enjoyed themselves again on their cherished steamboat trips along the rivers and canals. The photo shows a boat traveling along the Landwehr Canal, not far from the Potsdamer Bridge. To the left stand the ruins of the "House of German Tourism" that was built in 1938 on the "Round Plaza" where the New National Gallery stands today. The men are wearing ties, reflecting the formality of the times.

▷ Menschen sitzen auf dem Sockel des eigentlichen Wahrzeichens der Stadt, der Berolina am Alexanderplatz. Die 7,5 Meter hohe Kolossalfigur war 1944 als »freiwillige Metallspende des Deutschen Volkes« eingeschmolzen worden. – Die Berliner liebten schon immer ihre Gartenlokale. So pilgerte man im Sommer 1946 in den »Kroll-Garten« am Platz der Republik. Im Schatten der Ruinen der Kroll-Oper wurde getanzt. Nach zwölf Jahren NS-Diktatur war so manches nachzuholen. Man adaptierte vor allen Dingen Amerikanisches.

▷ *People are sitting on the base of what is the true symbol of the city, the Berolina at Alexanderplatz. The large 7.5 meter high figure was melted down in 1944 as the "German people's voluntary donation of metal." – The Berliners have always loved their garden cafés, which is why in the summer of 1946 they made a pilgrimage to the "Kroll Garten" at the Platz der Republik and danced in the shadows of the Kroll Opera ruins. There was a lot of catching up to do after twelve years of Nazi dictatorship. And they adapted everything American.*

1952

Juli 1946

1951

23. März 1949

Nach der Währungsreform veränderte sich das Leben im Westteil der Stadt zusehends. Zwar waren die Kriegsfolgen noch lange nicht behoben, doch völlig neu waren zum Beispiel die Bananenverkäufer, die vom LKW herunter ihre Ware verkauften. – Geldwechsler in der Hardenbergstraße. Mit der Einführung der sogenannten Westmark am 24.6.1948 begann das Geschäft der Geldwechsler, denn nun gab es in den westlichen Sektoren eine Doppelwährung, die den Schwarzmarkt förderte. Für eine Westmark bekam man vier bis sieben Ostmark.

After the new currency was introduced, life visibly changed in the western part of the city. The effects of the war were not yet gone, but brand new things emerged, like banana merchants selling their goods from trucks. – Money changers on Hardenbergstrasse. When the West Mark was introduced on June 24, 1948, the business with money changers began. There were now two currencies in the western sectors, adding a boost to the black market. For one West Mark you could get anywhere from four to seven East Marks.

▷ Kinder begießen sich in der Budapester Straße, im Schatten der Kaiser-Wilhelm-Gedächtniskirche, ausgelassen mit Wasser (oben); Kinder spielen mit Modell-»Rosinenbombern« Luftbrücke (unten). Für die Kriegskinder, wie sie später genannt wurden, waren die Jahre des Schreckens zwar nicht zu tilgen, doch trotz des Hungers und der Not genossen sie das Neue in vollen Zügen. Sie waren es, die in den 60er und 70er Jahren vehement gegen Kriege protestieren und sich für neue Gesellschaftsformen einsetzen sollten.

▷ *Children frolic in the water on Budapester Strasse, in the shadow of the Kaiser Wilhelm Memorial Church (above); Children play with model planes of the "Raisin Bomber" airlift (below). For the children of the war, as they were later called, it wasn't possible to erase the memory of the terror of these years of war, but despite hunger and poverty they still fully enjoyed everything new. Later, in the 60s and 70s, they would vehemently protest against war and fight for new forms of society.*

3. August 1954

1948 / 1949

4. August 1945

August 1953

19. November 1951

August 1946

Normalität setzt ein nach den Drangsalen von Diktatur und Krieg: In einer vom Bezirk Steglitz eingerichteten Nähstube werden aus Reststoffen Kleidungsstücke gefertigt (oben links); Skatspieler in einer Parkanlage (oben rechts); im Bendler-Block in Tiergarten werden Plakate hergestellt, die auf die amerikanische Wirtschaftshilfe im Rahmen des »Marshall-Plans« zum Wiederaufbau Europas hinweisen (unten links); eine sogenannte Kochmaschine, links im Bild, erleichterte in vielen Haushalten die Küchenarbeit (unten rechts).

Normality finally sets in after the hardships of dictatorship and the Second World War: In a sewing salon set up in the Steglitz district, clothing is made out of left-over material (above left); Card players playing a game of skat in a park (above right); in the Bendler Block in Tiergarten posters are printed publicizing the American economic aid to rebuild Europe through the Marshall Plan (below left); a so-called cooking machine, at left in photo, alleviated kitchen chores in many homes (below right).

▷ Nach den Jahren des nationalsozialistischen Schreckens und des Weltkriegs genossen die Kinder den Frieden, der ihnen auch einen regelmäßigen Schulbesuch ermöglichte. Auf den Fotos sehen wir eine Schulklasse mit Lehrerin in Lichterfelde-Süd beim Strickunterricht (oben) und Schulkinder vor ihrer Schule in der Levetzowstraße in Moabit (unten). Die meisten Ranzen waren noch aus Pappe – was bei nassem Wetter zu Problemen führte –, die Essenstöpfe waren für die Schulspeisung gedacht, die in den Pausen ausgegeben wurde.

▷ *After the long years of National Socialist terror and the Second World War, children enjoyed the peace that allowed them to attend school regularly. The photos show us schoolchildren with their teacher during knitting class in Lichterfelde Süd (above) and students standing in front of their school on Levetzowstrasse in Moabit (below). Most of the knapsacks were still made of paper – which was a problem when it rained; the pots were for the warm meals served at school during the break.*

17. November 1950

13. November 1952

27. Juni 1949

18. Januar 1953

Nach der Währungsreform wurde die Teilung der Stadt zunehmend spürbar, zum Beispiel beim Straßenbahnverkehr. Seit dem 24.3.1949 kam es an zwölf Grenzstellen zu einem Schaffnerwechsel, d.h. der Westgeld kassierende Schaffner durfte nicht in den Ostsektor fahren und vice versa. Hier sehen wir Personal der BVG West in einem als Wartehalle dienenden Autobus an der Ecke Potsdamer Straße / Linkstraße. – Derselbe Ort nach der Unterbrechung des Straßenbahndurchgangsverkehrs am 15.1.1953 auf Befehl der Ost-Berliner Behörde.

The currency reform made the division of the city more apparent, for example in streetcar transportation. Starting in March 24, 1949, drivers were switched at twelve border stops because a conductor who collected west money was not permitted to drive to the eastern sectors and vice versa. Here we see the public transportation staff in the West waiting in a bus at the corner of Potsdamer Strasse / Links trasse. – The same corner after the East Berlin authorities stopped streetcar traffic from passing through the eastern sections of the city.

▷ Am 20.3.1949 verfügten die westlichen Besatzungsmächte die Einführung der DM-West als allein gültiges Zahlungsmittel in den Westsektoren. Hier verlässt West-Berlins Oberbürgermeister Ernst Reuter die Stadtverordnetenversammlung im Hotel am Zoo nach der Verlesung der Verordnung über die neue Währung. – Fruchtlose Versuche, über die Probleme der geteilten Stadt zu diskutieren: Der Präsident des West-Berliner Abgeordnetenhauses, Willy Brandt, nimmt ein Schreiben des Oberbürgermeisters von Ost-Berlin, Friedrich Ebert, entgegen.

▷ *On March 20, 1949, the Western occupying powers ordered that the West Mark be the only valid form of payment in the western sectors. Here Ernst Reuter, mayor of West Berlin, is leaving the city council assembly in the Hotel am Zoo after he heard the orders concerning the new currency. – Fruitless attempts to discuss the problems of the divided city: Willy Brandt, former president of the West Berlin parliament, accepts a letter from Friedrich Ebert, mayor of East Berlin.*

20. März 1949

28. April 1956

23. Dezember 1959

Am 27.5.1952 unterbrach die Ost-Berliner Postbehörde sämtliche Telefonverbindungen zwischen dem östlichen und westlichen Teil Berlins. Eine bescheidene Erleichterung für die Ost-Berliner war die Aufstellung von Telefonzellen in Grenznähe – wie hier auf der Straße des 17. Juni, unmittelbar am Brandenburger Tor – und besonderen Sprechstellen in West-Berliner Postämtern, von denen aus Bewohner von Ost-Berlin und der DDR für DM-Ost Gespräche mit West-Berliner Bürgern führen konnten.

On May 27, 1952, the East Berlin postal authority broke off all telephone connections between the eastern and western sections of Berlin. A number of telephone booths put up close to the border, such as the one pictured here on Strasse des 17. Juni, not far from the Brandenburg Gate, provided a modest help to East Berliners. Special speaking stations in West Berlin post offices made it possible for residents of East Berlin and East Germany to call West Berliners using East Marks.

▷ Schmerzhafte Schnittstelle zwischen Ost und West: Aus dem einst so prächtigen Potsdamer Platz ist ein von Ruinen (rechts Pschorrhaus, im Hintergrund »Haus Vaterland«) gesäumtes »Dreiländereck« zwischen Sowjetischem, Amerikanischem und Britischem Sektor gewachsen. – Am benachbarten Leipziger Platz suggerieren die Oberleitungen, hier würde noch die Straßenbahn fahren. Doch die Schienen sind bereits von Wildkräutern überwuchert. Im Hintergrund stützt ein Gerüst die Ruine des Warenhauses Wertheim, die 1957 abgerissen wurde.

▷ *A painful gateway between the East and West: Potsdamer Platz, once so magnificent, has now become a triangle of ruins (the Pschorrhaus at the right, Haus Vaterland seen in back) enclosed by the Soviet, American and British sectors. – At the nearby Leipziger Platz overhead cables give the impression that the streetcars still run here. But the tracks are overgrown with wild herbs. In the background scaffolding supports the ruins of the Wertheim department store that was torn down in 1957.*

11. April 1951

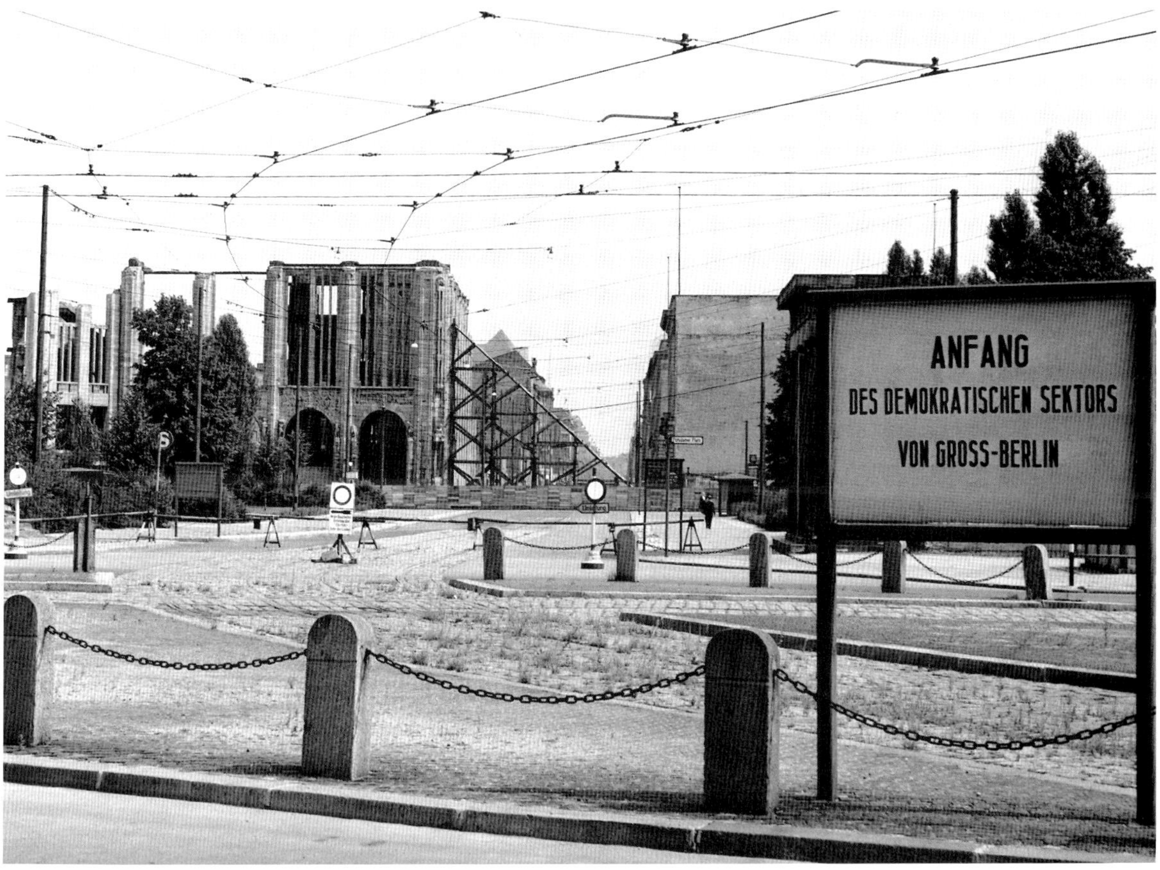

6. August 1956

1953

1958

12. Februar 1954

1957

Auch in der Baukunst entfernten sich Ost und West voneinander. Die Frankfurter Allee, ab 1949 Stalinallee, wurde ab 1952 zur ersten »sozialistischen Straße Deutschlands« im Architekturstil der Stalin-Ära wiederaufgebaut (links oben und unten). Im Westen machte unterdessen das »demokratische Bauen« Furore. So entstand 1956 bis 1958 an der Heilsberger Allee nahe des Olympiastadions das Le-Corbusier-Haus (rechts oben). Zur Internationalen Bauausstellung wurde im Hansa-Viertel diese Musterwohnung gezeigt (rechts unten).

▷ Im Osten Berlins wurden schon bald die meisten Läden durch die 1948 gegründete staatliche Handelsorganisation, kurz HO genannt, kontrolliert, die in Konkurrenz zu der genossenschaftlich geführten Konsum-Kette stand und von Regierungsseite bevorteilt wurde. Das Foto zeigt das Schaufenster eines HO-Warenhauses mit reichhaltigem alkoholischem Angebot. Auch dies ist typisch für die 50er Jahre: Selbst die Warenauslage bleibt im sozialistischen Teil der Stadt nicht verschont von politischer Propaganda.

East and West grew in different directions in their architecture, too. The Frankfurter Allee, called Stalinallee by 1949, was reconstructed in 1952 into the first "Socialist street in Germany," using the architectural style of the Stalin era (left above and below). Meanwhile, in the West "democratic building" was causing a sensation. The Le Corbusier House (above right) emerged from 1956 to 1958 on Heilsberger Allee, near the Olympic Stadium. This model apartment was shown at the International Building Exhibition in the Hansa Quarter (below right).

▷ *In East Berlin most stores were soon controlled by the state-run trade organization that was founded in 1948 and abbreviated as HO. These shops were favored by the government and competed with the collectively-run Konsum chain stores. In this photo we see the shop window of an HO store with a large display of alcohol. And also typical of the fifties: Even the display of merchandise in the socialist section of the city is not free of political propaganda. The poster says: "Save Ethel and Julius Rosenberg."*

RETTET
Ethel und Julius
Rosenberg
JEDE STIMME ZÄHLT! EILE TUT NOT!
HO
HO
11.-
13.-
16.-
14.-
12.-
32.-
45.-
8.-

um 1955

Januar 1953

Auch in jenen Jahren nach dem Krieg blieb das Schlittenfahren eine der schönsten Winterfreuden – für Kinder und Erwachsene gleichermaßen. Die Fotografie zeigt Kriegskinder im schneereichen Winter 1952 / 53 auf der Rodelbahn am Kreuzberg in dem Bezirk gleichen Namens. Im Hintergrund des Bildes ist das von Karl Friedrich Schinkel entworfene Nationaldenkmal für die Befreiungskriege zu erkennen. Das prachtvolle Denkmal war 1821 eingeweiht und 1878 auf einen acht Meter hohen Sockel gehoben worden.

▷ Auch Weihnachtsmärkte gehörten zu den Winterfreuden. Fand im Westteil der Stadt der Markt an der Ruine der Kaiser-Wilhelm-Gedächtniskirche statt (oben), so wurde im Ostteil Weihnachten, hier als »Friedensweihnacht« fungierend, im Schatten der Schlossruine gefeiert: auf dem Marx-Engels-Platz, dem ehemaligen Lustgarten, nach dem Abriss des Schlosses um dessen Areal erweitert. Als der West-Berliner Markt später in die Messehallen am Funkturm verlegt wurde, gingen die Besucherzahlen spürbar zurück.

Even during these first years after the world war, sledding remained one of the great pleasures of winter – for both children and adults alike. The photograph shows children of the war in the snowy winter of 1952 / 53 on the toboggan run at the Kreuzberg, a hill named after the district. The Wars of Liberation national monument designed by Karl Friedrich can be seen in the background. This grand monument was dedicated in 1821 and raised onto an eight meter high base in 1878.

▷ *Christmas markets were also one of the joys of winter. In the western part of the city the market took place at the ruins of the Kaiser Wilhelm Memorial Church (above), in the eastern part of the city Christmas was celebrated as the first peacetime Christmas after the war in the shadow of the palace ruins, on the Marx-Engels Plaza, the former Lustgarten, extended to include the grounds of the palace after it was torn down. When the West Berlin market was later moved to the convention hall at the radio tower, the number of visitors declined.*

Dezember 1951

1954

1949

Mit der Aufhebung der Blockade am 12. Mai 1949 ging im Westen ein Traum der Bevölkerung in Erfüllung. Ein weiterer Schritt zur Normalisierung des Lebens wurde getan. Die Schaufenster und Regale der Geschäfte füllten sich im Westteil der Stadt mit Waren des täglichen Bedarfs, vor allem mit den bis dahin knappen Lebensmitteln. Mit großen Augen wurden die Angebote beäugt und die Preise verglichen. Für üppige Einkäufe fehlte allerdings in den meisten Haushalten noch das nötige Geld.

When the blockade was lifted on May 12, 1949 a dream came true for the population in the West. Another step towards normality had been achieved. Shop windows and shelves in the western part of the city were filled with everyday goods, most importantly food that until then had been scarce. People gazed in amazement at the large selections of merchandise in the stores and began to compare prices. But it would be a long time before most families could afford many of the attractive goods on display.

▷ Vor einem HO-Warenhaus in der Stalinallee, 1961 in Karl-Marx-Allee umbenannt, im Bezirk Friedrichshain wird an einem Imbissstand die berühmte Bratwurst verkauft. – Ein einschneidendes Ereignis für die West-Berliner war die Wiedereröffnung des Kaufhaus des Westens am 3.7.1950. Das berühmte Warenhaus war während des Krieges schwer beschädigt worden. Dass das KaDeWe und andere bekannte Kaufhäuser und Geschäfte schon bald wieder Waren feilboten, ließ das nahende »Wirtschaftswunder« erahnen.

▷ *In front of the state-run trade organization store on Stalinallee, renamed Karl-Marx-Allee in 1961, in the district of Friedrichshain, the famous bratwurst is sold at a snack bar. – An important event for West Berliners was the re-opening of the Kaufhaus des Westens on July 3, 1950. The famous department store was badly damaged during the war. That KaDeWe and other well-known department stores were soon able to offer merchandise again was a hint of the upcoming "economic miracle."*

1959

3. Juli 1950

September 1953

4. Juli 1956

September 1953

30. Juni 1954

Bilder des Nachkriegsalltags in West-Berlin: Badegäste am Strandbad Wannsee (oben links); die Imbissbude des »Dicken Heinrich« an der Wilmersdorfer Straße, in unmittelbarer Nähe des Kurfürstendammes, an der sich bis zum frühen Morgen die Nachtbummler trafen (oben rechts); Entspannung im eigenen Wohnwagen, aufgestellt am Postfenn im Grunewald (unten links); Straßenbahn an der belebten Ecke Kurfürstendamm / Uhlandstraße am letzten Tag vor Einstellung der Linie 76 – Auto und Autobus schienen zeitgemäßer (unten rechts).

Pictures of daily life in postwar West Berlin: Swimmers at the Wannsee lake beach; the snack bar "Dicken Heinrich" on Wilmersdorfer Strasse, right off of Kurfürstendamm, where customers came from early morning till the late hours of the night (above right); relaxing in their personal trailer home parked at Postfenn in Grunewald (below left); a street car at the corner of Kurfürstendamm / Uhlandstrasse on the last day of Line 76 – cars and busses were deemed more modern (below right).

▷ Berlin, Kurfürstendamm – das war ab den 50er Jahren ein Synonym für: Boulevard der Filmtheater. Lange Warteschlangen vor den Kinokassen gehörten zum alltäglichen Bild. Hier, in der »Film-Bühne Wien«, wird Willy Forsts Streifen »Die Sünderin« mit Hildegard Knef und Gustav Fröhlich gezeigt. Über drei Millionen Zuschauer in Deutschland sahen sich den Film an – nicht zuletzt wegen einer kurzen Nacktszene der Knef, die von jetzt an zu den Stars des deutschen Kinos gezählt wurde.

▷ *Berlin, Kurfürstendamm – that was a synonym in the fifties for the movie mile. Waiting in long lines to buy tickets for a showing was a part of everyday life at the time. Here the "Film Bühne Wien," a popular movie house on the avenue, is showing Willy Forst's flick "The Story of a Sinner" starring Hildegard Knef and Gustav Fröhlich in the main roles. Over three million people in Germany saw the film when it first came out, no doubt thanks to Knef's nude scene, which later established her as German film star.*

Meisterwerk
Die Sünderin
HILDEGARD KNEF
GUSTAV FRÖHLICH
FILM-BÜHNE WIEN

März 1951